The College Student's Guide to Writing A Great Research Paper

101 Easy Tips & Tricks to Make Your Work Stand Out

BY ERIKA EBY

The College Student's Guide to Writing A Great Research Paper:
101 Easy Tips & Tricks to Make Your Work Stand Out

Library of Congress Cataloging-in-Publication Data

Eby, Erika, 1988-
  The college student's guide to writing a great research paper : 101 easy tips & tricks to make your work stand out / by Erika Eby.
      p. cm.
  Includes bibliographical references and index.
  ISBN-13: 978-1-60138-605-2 (alk. paper)
  ISBN-10: 1-60138-605-2 (alk. paper)
  1. English language--Rhetoric. 2. Report writing. I. Title.
  PE1408.E296 2011
  808.06'6378--dc23

                                        2011031417

Printed in the United States

PROJECT MANAGER: Gretchen Pressley • gpressley@atlantic-pub.com
ASSISTANT EDITOR & PROOFREADER: Alyssa Appelman • alyssa.appelman@gmail.com
BOOK PRODUCTION DESIGN: T.L. Price • design@tlpricefreelance.com
FRONT/BACK COVER DESIGN: Jackie Miller • millerjackiej@gmail.com

Printed on Recycled Paper

A few years back we lost our beloved pet dog Bear, who was not only our best and dearest friend but also the "Vice President of Sunshine" here at Atlantic Publishing. He did not receive a salary but worked tirelessly 24 hours a day to please his parents.

Bear was a rescue dog who turned around and showered myself, my wife, Sherri, his grandparents Jean, Bob, and Nancy, and every person and animal he met (well, maybe not rabbits) with friendship and love. He made a lot of people smile every day.

We wanted you to know a portion of the profits of this book will be donated in Bear's memory to local animal shelters, parks, conservation organizations, and other individuals and nonprofit organizations in need of assistance.

– Douglas & Sherri Brown

PS: We have since adopted two more rescue dogs: first Scout, and the following year, Ginger. They were both mixed golden retrievers who needed a home.

Want to help animals and the world? Here are a dozen easy suggestions you and your family can implement today:

- *Adopt and rescue a pet from a local shelter.*
- *Support local and no-kill animal shelters.*
- *Plant a tree to honor someone you love.*
- *Be a developer — put up some birdhouses.*
- *Buy live, potted Christmas trees and replant them.*
- *Make sure you spend time with your animals each day.*
- *Save natural resources by recycling and buying recycled products.*
- *Drink tap water, or filter your own water at home.*
- *Whenever possible, limit your use of or do not use pesticides.*
- *If you eat seafood, make sustainable choices.*
- *Support your local farmers market.*
- *Get outside. Visit a park, volunteer, walk your dog, or ride your bike.*

Five years ago, Atlantic Publishing signed the Green Press Initiative. These guidelines promote environmentally friendly practices, such as using recycled stock and vegetable-based inks, avoiding waste, choosing energy-efficient resources, and promoting a no-pulping policy. We now use 100-percent recycled stock on all our books. The results: in one year, switching to post-consumer recycled stock saved 24 mature trees, 5,000 gallons of water, the equivalent of the total energy used for one home in a year, and the equivalent of the greenhouse gases from one car driven for a year.

Table of Contents

Introduction **13**

Using This Book 15

Chapter 1: Before You Begin............... 17

What is a Research Paper? 17

Types of Research Papers....................................... 18

Questions to Ask Before Starting a Paper 19

**Chapter 2: Prewriting
and Getting Started.............................. 25**

Myths about Prewriting 25

Benefits of prewriting 27

Mind Mapping or Clustering.................................. 29

Visual connection or web of ideas 30

Interrelated concepts to branch from general concept...... 31

Free writing 33

   First thoughts that come to mind 34

   No consideration or restraints on grammar
and mechanics 34

   Why this method is effective 36

Brainstorming and Listing 36

   Randomly generating ideas 36

   Listing any ideas that come to mind on the topic 37

Why These Techniques Work 39

Case Study: Importance of Prewriting 40

Chapter 3: Narrowing Your Focus and Developing a Thesis Statement 45

Finding a Broad Focus, and Narrowing it Down 46

   How to narrow the focus 47

Developing a Thesis Statement 52

   Creating the frame: Turning a topic into a thesis 53

   Message and purpose 54

   Declarative statement 55

   A direction 56

   A hook 57

   Clear, concise writing 59

   Choosing the right words 61

Thesis Statement Examples 63

Case Study: Thesis Statements and Great Papers 68

Chapter 4: Research............................71

Case Study: Researching like a Professional.......................... 72

Finding Credible Sources 75

    Examining source credentials and affiliations................... 76

    Evaluating for areas of bias 79

    Other things to consider.. 83

Using the Library... 86

    Using books, references, and periodicals 87

Using Online Library Databases 90

    How to select and search online databases 91

Using the Internet... 94

    Types of websites... 94

    Wikipedia 95

    Using a blog as a resource.. 98

    Determining trustworthiness of Internet information...... 99

Case Study: A Scientist's Perspective 101

Chapter 5: Organizing and Outlining...105

Organizing Information and Sources 105

Notecards 106

Notecard example 109

Developing An Outline 110

Why developing an outline is important 111

How to construct an outline.. 112

Topic outline 114

Sample topic outline 114

Sentence outline 116

Sentence outline sample 117

Quotation outline... 120

Chapter 6: Plagiarism and Using Research in a Paper................. 125

Plagiarism and its Consequences.. 125

What is plagiarism? 126

The consequences.. 126

Case Study: Avoiding Plagiarism....................................... 129

Quoting... 130

When to use a quotation 131

Citations and quoting 131

Paraphrasing 132

When to use a paraphrase.. 134

Citations and paraphrasing.. 135

Summarizing 136

    When to use a summary.. 137

    Citations and summarizing 138

Chapter 7: Citation Methods 143

MLA Format 146

    The MLA in-text citation 147

    Sample MLA citations.. 147

APA Format... 148

    The APA in-text citation... 148

    Sample APA citations 149

Turabian or Chicago Style...................................... 151

    The Chicago/Turabian in-text citation........................ 151

    Sample Chicago/Turabian in-text citations.................. 152

Case Study: Learning Styles and Asking for Assistance........ 154

Chapter 8: Writing the Introduction 159

What to Include 160

    Writing the hook.. 161

    Providing background information.............................. 163

    Previewing key points for the rest of paper.................. 167

    Leading into the thesis statement 168

Effective Introduction Techniques.. 169

Sample Introduction 173

Chapter 9: Writing the Body of Your Paper 177

Support Thesis Claims 178

Use details for support.. 179

Use cited research 181

Substantiate information with credible research............. 181

Include proper citations... 184

Develop a Rhythm... 185

Follow Outline and Thesis Statement................................. 187

Flow neatly from one topic to the next.......................... 189

Case Study: Advice From a College Prep Teacher................ 193

Chapter 10: Wrapping Things Up with the Conclusion 197

Effective Conclusion Techniques... 199

Restate the thesis 201

Review or reiterate key points.. 202

Provide resolution 203

Traps to Avoid 204

Too much summarization.. 204

Introduction of new information.................................... 205

Sample Conclusion 207

Case Study: Great Conclusions Make For Great Papers....... 209

Chapter 11: Formatting and Reference Pages 213

Formatting the Paper 214

    Finding formatting requirements.................................... 214

    How to adjust the format 215

    Headers and Footers... 216

Reference Pages.. 217

    What is a reference page?.. 218

    The importance of reference pages................................ 219

MLA Works Cited 220

    Sample 220

APA Reference Page 221

    Sample 222

Chicago or Turabian Bibliography 223

    Sample 224

Chapter 12: Proofreading and Editing 227

Reading for Content.. 228

Thesis properly supported 229

All research objectives met................................ 232

Case Study: Editing tips from the Writing Center 235

Grammar, Spelling, and Mechanics.......................... 236

Proofing for errors in basic grammar and mechanics...... 237

Using automated grammar and spell-checkers 241

Other Resources for Polishing a Paper........................ 243

Conclusion: The Road to Success is a Rocky One 247

Case Study: Senior Advice 249

Appendix A: Sample Research Papers......251

Appendix B: Helpful Links......273

Appendix C: Glossary 275

Author Biography......283

Index......285

Introduction

If you are anything like I was, getting ready for college involves a roller coaster of emotions along with met and unmet expectations. Leaving home and taking a huge leap into adulthood is scary, but with it comes a huge surge of excitement.

After spending countless hours filling out college applications and making sure to highlight each achievement and stand out from the crowd as much as possible, I had chosen — and even better been accepted into — a prestigious university at which to earn my degree. Armed with a laptop, notebooks, pens, dorm room supplies, and coffee for late-night study sessions, I faced the transition from high school academics to college. I felt ready for whatever these new classes could throw at me.

Once the classes started, however, reality began to eat away at some of my enthusiasm. For me, the stress of classes set in about the same time the novelty of living in a dorm room wore off — which just happened to be the third time the circuit breaker blew because a neighbor was drying her hair while I was using the microwave.

For a beginning college student, adjusting to lectures and the workload can be difficult. The first week of classes was great, but by week three, I was looking at three separate papers with looming deadlines, all of which were in the same week. I took college prep classes in high school but still felt overwhelmed; my friends who had not been so prepared felt even more so. I had no idea how to impress any of my professors or know what they were expecting or even where to start.

Ready to rip my hair out, I stared forlornly at a blank word processing screen. That I was an English major, someone who was supposed to be good at this sort of thing, only added insult to injury. Trying to balance classes, part-time work, extracurriculars, and a social life is difficult enough. Putting together what my professors considered a simple assignment should have been a breeze, but this often was not the case.

The sad truth is stories like mine are not uncommon. Many students feel they do not receive guidance about college, and it can be difficult to distinguish yourself from the masses of other students. This is especially true at larger universities with enormous lecture halls. Students who are used to receiving personal attention to their work become frustrated with trying to get noticed. The only time to impress a professor with the same intelligence, hard work, and dedication that got you accepted to college often is through written assignments, but many professors read hundreds of papers for a class. Even smaller colleges are generally larger than most high schools, which can make standing out tough. This means if you want to catch someone's eye, you have to avoid common pitfalls and turn in an excellent research paper. As daunting as this prospect might seem, it is an invaluable way to make sure your professors sit up and take notice.

For students who have difficulty writing or are new to writing college papers, this can be a nerve-racking idea. Whether you consider yourself a struggling writer, a newcomer to the college writing scene, or a skilled writer looking for more ways to enhance your writing, this book can help. Writing papers does not have to involve hours of staring at a blank screen and wondering where to start, and with practice, writing research papers can become a simple and painless process. By using the available resources, I got over my nervousness and writer's block and started turning out papers in no time. By my senior year, I was impressing professors with my projects. Now, I am here to share with you some of the tips and tricks I picked up from students, professors, and fellow writers so you can enjoy the same success.

Using This Book

This book is designed to provide college students at any skill level with the tools they need to put together a research paper that will attract the right kind of attention and earn them praise and excellent grades. The book covers prewriting, researching, and outlining and drafting an introduction, body, and conclusion. This book will guide you through the steps to writing a paper with punch. Each chapter will provide useful tips and tricks to aid you with each stage of the writing process.

In addition to drafting a paper, the book covers formatting or typesetting and understanding plagiarism. Formatting and citation can be tricky. This book will explain multiple common methods for citing sources and when and how to use them. Improper citations could lead to lost points on assignments, but if they lead to plagiarism accusations, you might also risk legal action and expulsion. Whether you need help with the entire writing process or just have a few trouble spots, this book is a guide to getting top grades and recognition from your professors on all your future assignments.

CHAPTER 1

Before You Begin

Whether you have seldom had to deal with research papers during your academic career or have been writing them for a while, there are a few important things to consider before diving into the writing process. Research papers come in all shapes and sizes, so understanding exactly what you are getting yourself into when starting a paper is crucial. The following sections offer basic information to consider as you begin the process of writing a research paper.

What is a Research Paper?

The majority of papers you will write in an academic setting will be research papers. Any paper requiring the writer to research a particular topic is a research paper. Unlike essays, which are often based largely on opinion and are written from the author's point of view, research papers are based in fact. Anecdotes and creative storytelling have no place inside a research paper. This is not to say research papers cannot be creative or contain the author's opinion. They should be, and they do. The big difference between a research paper and many other forms of writing is research papers force the writer to back up their opinions and assertions with facts found through thorough research on a given topic. They force students to form an opinion on a topic, research that topic, and then showcase that knowledge by writing about it. Because of this, they are a staple in almost every subject within the academic world.

Tip No. 1 Research papers force you to form an opinion on a topic and then back it up with facts.

You can try to be creative in your presentation, but research papers rely on facts found through research to construct a logical and compelling argument.

Types of Research Papers

There are several types of research papers. Some research papers are short, and some are in-depth. Everything from a three-page literary analysis to a 40-page senior analysis is a research paper. The beauty of research papers is they all follow the same basic structure whether you are writing a summary of scientific research conducted over the course of a semester, analyzing a novel, or drawing conclusions from several psychological studies. The tips found in this book can apply to any research paper you write.

Tip No. 2 Research papers of all types have almost identical structures at their core.

There will be some basic differences, but if you can write one type of research paper, you can write another. Do not let literary criticism intimidate you if you are a chemistry major or scientific research scare you if you are an English major.

Although you can apply the same basic structure and tips to just about any research paper, some stylistic rules will vary from subject to subject. Familiarity with MLA format will help you with that English paper, but it might not help with a chemistry analysis. *Chapter 7 will provide more information on formatting your paper and using different styles for various types of research papers.*

Tip No. **3** Familiarize yourself with different formats for writing papers.

Having a passing knowledge of multiple styles will make them much less intimidating if you happen to run across them at a later date.

Questions to Ask Before Starting a Paper

Now you have a solid understanding of what a research paper is, make sure you have all the information you need to write the best possible paper for a given assignment. Often, professors will give out a rubric or assignment sheet with all the information you need to know about an assignment, but this is not always the case.

Tip No. **4** Do not put off reading over assignments for research papers.

Few things are worse than ignoring a huge project until the last minute and then realizing you do not understand part of it. It often is too late to get clarification at that point, so read those assignment sheets immediately upon receiving them.

Sometimes you do not receive a clear list of instructions. This can be especially frustrating for students as they flounder through an assignment because they aren't sure of what is expected of them or whether they are doing the assignment correctly. Asking your professor for clarification on specific points before starting an assignment will save you a lot of fuss and headache later during the writing process. If your professor is unavailable, your classmates can often help. Many schools also have tutors or writing centers available to help students with papers, so use these resources. Always check the class syllabus or website, if possible, to determine whether any additional information is there.

Tip No. 5 Ask questions about an assignment until you are sure you have a handle on it.

Many students needlessly lose points on assignments because they did not understand every aspect of it. Ask questions, get clarification, and do not wait until the last minute to do so. You might find help is unavailable later but would have been earlier.

The following is a list of questions you should ask either yourself or your professor before beginning any paper:

- **Are there any requirements for the topic of the paper?**
  Professors will often provide a general theme for an assignment and expect students to pick a topic relating to that theme.

- **Are any subjects off-limits for this paper?** A professor might say one or two topics covered within the class should not be included in any papers. They might also have a list of topics that they see too often and recommend students avoid.

- **How long should the paper be?** This is important because the length of a paper will change which topics you can adequately cover within the assignment. Some professors will not give a set length for an assignment, but most will at least recommend a page or word count. Make sure you have this information so you can plan the paper accordingly.

- **Which format should the paper be in?** There are several different styles or formats in which to write a paper. *Chapter 7 will give more information about a paper's format.* Be sure you know in which format your professor is expecting to receive the paper so you can brush up on that format.

- **Is a number of sources required?** Professors could set a minimum number of sources for a paper or have a rough expectation of how many sources are appropriate for a research paper. Not having the proper number of sources is a petty thing to lose points over, so make sure you are aware of any requirements. Choose a topic that lets you meet any requirements in this department.

- **Are any types of sources restricted?** Professors might restrict certain types of sources for a given assignment. Most commonly, professors will restrict the number or type of Internet sources used in an assignment. Other restrictions might also apply, so always ask.

- **Should you turn in any additional materials with the paper?** Some assignments might require you to turn in multiple drafts of the same paper, turn in a cover page or an outline, or include a certain number of charts or graphs with your paper. Most professors will make this clear when this is the case, but always ask for clarification if you have any questions so you know you are turning in the correct materials.

- **Does the professor have any other specific requirements for the paper?** Every professor is different, and they often have their own requirements for how they want things done. They might require you to print your paper in a specific font or print your pages double-sided. When professors have odd or specific, nonstandard expectations for papers, they make them clear in the class syllabus or on an assignment sheet, but always ask for clarification if you have any doubt or are confused.

Study Guide

- Research papers are a staple of any academic discipline.

- Research papers require students to form an opinion on a topic and then back up their assertions about the subject with facts found through research.

- Although different types of research papers might require different formats and will cover varying subjects, much of the basic structure and the tips for improvement are universal.

- Because there are many things to consider when writing a research paper, do not be afraid to ask questions and get all of the important information you need before you begin writing and researching.

- Use all the resources your campus has available if you have trouble understanding an assignment and your professor is unavailable.

CHAPTER 2

Prewriting and Getting Started

Most students let out a collective groan whenever prewriting for an assignment is mentioned. For whichever reason, sitting down and writing to get ideas is a turnoff for many students. Few realize how vital this step is to the writing process and then wonder why they keep getting stuck when they sit down to crank out that paper. Students feel as though they were brimming with ideas while they were mulling over their assignments, but nothing comes out when the time comes to write the words down in a neat, coherent manner. This is when prewriting comes in and is exactly why it is so important to the writing process. Prewriting gets all those loose ideas down on paper so they can be organized and not forgotten when the time to begin writing comes.

Myths about Prewriting

Tip No. 6

Do not dismiss prewriting.
Prewriting is a vital part of the writing process and a way to generate and organize ideas so you do not forget them. Prewrite at least a small amount before any research paper.

The most common myths about prewriting probably are it is not necessary and it takes extra time students cannot afford to give up. Many students have a false concept of what it means to prewrite, which is why they so quickly dismiss it. The human thought process is disorganized and nebulous. Without prewriting, students sort through chaotic ideas while they are writing rather than have neat thoughts around which to structure a paper. This is difficult and only creates more work for students. The time you do not spend staring at your computer wondering what to write next will make up for the time you lose prewriting.

Tip No. **7 Prewriting saves time. It does not waste it.**
It can be tempting to say you do not have time to prewrite, but prewriting will help you select a topic more quickly and will help you sort through the mess of ideas in your head, which will save time later.

Another common myth is prewriting needs to be good or organized. This is not the case. Several methods of prewriting exist, but the purpose of prewriting is to get ideas and concepts whether good or bad down on paper. Once these rough notes are written down, they can be organized for later. Bad ideas can be tossed out, and what seems to be a bad or useless idea can spark an idea or thought that turns into a basis for a paper.

Tip No. **8 Do not be afraid to let your prewriting be messy.**
This is not the paper yet, and the time for neatness will come later. Right now, getting those ideas on paper is more important.

Students might also have tried one particular method of prewriting that they did not find helpful, so they dismiss prewriting. There are as many types of prewriting as there are types of students. This chapter discusses three common methods, but students should experiment and find which works best for them. You might find your prewriting needs more or less structure to it. You can combine prewriting methods or make up your own, but this chapter will give you ideas for what prewriting should accomplish.

Benefits of prewriting

The ultimate goal of prewriting is to save time and frustration later during the writing process. Prewriting allows writers to quickly record a large quantity of ideas to later organize into a solid paper topic. Prewriting allows students to narrow their paper topics from broad ideas to specifics and figure out which key points to address within those specific ideas. Writers who do some sort of prewriting activity are less likely to get stuck while typing out the bulk of their papers. They are also much less likely to forget ideas they had planned to include in their papers.

Prewriting is especially useful when dealing with broad or ambiguous research assignments. Classes might assign specific topics for research papers, but assignments often are general. For example, your professor might tell you to research something covered during your semester in ancient history and write a five- to seven-page paper on it. In instances like this, students have a few interesting ideas but no direction when they sit down to begin researching or writing. Prewriting will help you generate a topic and give you ideas for backup topics in case your research reveals a problem with your original idea.

> **Tip No. 10** **Prewriting can help you choose a topic *and* give you ideas for what to write about that topic.**
> Prewriting is a way to figure out which topics would work best for your paper and determine how ideas within that topic are connected, which will form the basis for your paper.

Prewriting allows students to make connections between ideas that they otherwise would not have. These connections are the stuff that excellent research papers are made of. Many papers on similar topics tend to cover the same points and read alike, so any uncommon ideas you come up with will make your paper more interesting than the majority of the papers that other students submit. Different, well-thought-out ideas are the first step to getting out of the slush pile of papers on your professor's desk.

> **Tip No. 11** **Embrace creative thinking and unique ideas at this stage.**
> You never know what will turn into a successful research paper, so embrace strange ideas or connections between topics as they come to you. These unique ideas can turn into papers your professor will enjoy reading.

Mind Mapping or Clustering

Human thought patterns are nebulous and not neatly organized. The mind's filing system is not alphabetical or chronological. Exactly how the mind groups memories is not fully understood, but things are grouped in a way that is much closer to categorical.

Our minds make connections between ideas or events in what seems to be random ways.

Tip No.

12 Even if your thoughts seem organized, they are not.

When people do not have a computer or notebook handy and are mulling over ideas, they seem to have many of them that flow neatly together. But ideas are nebulous and loosely connected. Mind mapping takes advantage of this by making a web of ideas that visually approximates the way your mind connects ideas.

Mind mapping or clustering takes advantage of this fact by helping you visually lay out concepts and ideas as you think of them in an organic, nonhierarchical way. Many students are already familiar with this technique though they might have heard it referred to as idea mapping, web diagramming, or something similar. These charts are helpful in organizing large amounts of information and bring together words and visual aids. For this reason, visual learners find this method of prewriting particularly effective.

Visual connection or web of ideas

Starting a mind map or cluster diagram is easy. These diagrams consist of clusters or branches of related information radiating from a central concept or idea. They look like a spider's web or the top view of a tree when completed. To create one of these diagrams you will need:

- A fresh sheet of paper that is at least 8.5-by-11 inches though larger is generally better, especially for students who have large handwriting
- A flat surface to spread out on
- A pen or pencil — optionally, students who enjoy color coding or have an artistic flare can use colored pens or markers

To begin working on the diagram, place the broad topic of the research paper you are working on in a circle or box at the center of the page. If you do not have a broad topic, use the first thing that comes to mind. If you have a specific idea in mind, use that. Add circles around your central idea containing other related thoughts. Connect these circles back to the central topic with lines. Each of these ideas will become a branch in the diagram. Branches can be anything, even ideas you are not interested in including in your paper.

Tip No. **13** Do not omit branches from your map.
It can be tempting to censor your thought map, but write down everything that comes to mind. You never know what will connect as the map progresses. Exercises like mind mapping work best when you let the ideas flow and connect without placing restrictions on yourself or the map.

Interrelated concepts to branch from general concept

Once a branch is started, continue to work on related concepts to that branch as they come to mind and make the branch longer. Branches can split into multiple subbranches where needed. Whenever the ideas start coming slowly, return to the main concept and begin a new branch. At any point, you can jump between branches to add things as they come to mind, but the goal is to get as many branches and as much information to work with as possible. If you are working with colored pens or markers, you can use a different color for ideas that stand out as useful or interesting to you. Doodles can be included as part of these maps if they help organize the information or make it easier to remember.

> **Tip No. 14 Get out the coloring supplies and have fun.**
>
> Mind mapping is especially effective for people who are visually oriented, but it can work for everyone. Because it is such a visual prewriting method, doodle and use an array of colors if it helps you sort through ideas. The more fun you have while making your map, the more relaxed you will be and the better your ideas will be.

Once you have several branches and many ideas pertaining to your topic, pulling back and looking at the diagram as a whole is a good idea. You might notice some overlap in concepts and topics covered in each individual branch. If it does not make the diagram too cluttered, draw connecting lines between areas of the diagram that could be connected in the paper. You might wish to do the same with points of comparison or contrast depending on which direction the research paper is going. If the diagram is already cluttered, copy it over more neatly onto another sheet of paper or just make notations to yourself in some of the blank space left on the page.

If you used the diagram to narrow a broad topic, pick out the particular branch or branches that seem to be the best choice to write the paper about. You might then do another web using the new narrower topic as the center of the map to generate specific ideas to research. If you started with a narrow topic, pick out the branches that seem to be the best choices to include in your paper.

The following is a sample mind map.

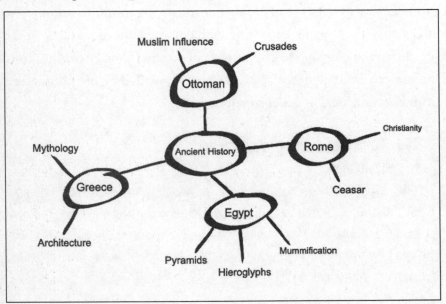

Tip No. 15 Once the map is complete, go back and prune.

After you have had time to look over the map and make notations, go back and choose the best ideas and bits of information to come out of the mapping session. Be discriminant and only choose the best ideas. If you do not like any of your ideas, you can always try again.

Free writing

Free writing is mind mapping's less visually oriented cousin. Like mind mapping, free writing relies heavily on getting ideas down on paper as they come to you and places quantity over quality. Unlike mind mapping, these ideas are not laid out visually. Instead, they are just written down as they come to mind in one large block. The goal of free writing is to force yourself to write a deluge of words that will later be edited and organized into a structured and coherent paper topic.

Free writes can be handwritten or typed. Handwritten free writes are much more common, but if being able to read your own quickly scribbled handwriting is a concern, typing might be a better choice. Free writing does not have to be a timed activity, but setting a timer in the beginning for three to five minutes is helps develop the habit.

Tip No. **16** Set time goals when you first begin free writing.

If you have issues forcing yourself to prewrite or are unsure how long to prewrite, use an egg timer or set an alarm on your cell phone for three to five minutes, and then write until it goes off.

First thoughts that come to mind

Start by writing the general topic at the top of the paper as a jumping-off point, and then write the first thoughts that come to mind. The goal of the free write should be to keep the words flowing for the entirety of the activity, even if that means writing the same word or phrase repeatedly until something else comes to mind. Tangents and unrelated thoughts are fine though attempt to get back to the main ideas as soon as possible. When unsure of what to write, it is fine to write, "I don't know what to write," or whatever else comes to mind when you think of your assignment. Again, the goal is quantity more than quality at this stage in the writing process.

No consideration or restraints on grammar and mechanics

Do not place too much emphasis on proper spelling, grammar, or mechanics while free writing. Punctuation is not necessary. Refrain from getting hung up on how to spell words or how to phrase ideas. Just keep writing ideas as they come to mind regardless of how you feel about them, and you eventually will find yourself writing down things that seem useful or interesting.

After the free write is complete, return to it with a critical eye. Underline or highlight any ideas that could turn into a topic for the paper or are specific points you know you will want to cover in the paper. As you pull these ideas out of the free write, make notations to yourself about any additional ideas that come to mind. All these ideas will eventually be reworked into an outline and thesis statement. The more you start with, the less work you will have later. Ideas can also be tossed out later in the research process if they turn out to be unhelpful or there is a lack of information on the topic.

The following is a sample free write.

<u>Ancient History Paper</u>

```
Man, I really don't know what to write.
I don't know what to do this paper
about...it seems really long and hard and
I don't really like ancient history that
much...ancient history ancient history
ancient history I saw a thing about
greek mythology on TV the other day but
it didn't really interest me so I don't
really want to write about that though
tomorrow there is supposed to be a show on
about Egypt... When I was a kid I use to
really like Egypt and I had lots of books
about mummies. Everyone does stuff about
mummies though so maybe there is something
else about Egypt I can do. Pyramids sphinx
giza nile crocodile hieroglyphs are neat.
Maybe I should look into the rosetta stone
and how hieroglyphs developed and how they
were eventually translated.
```

Why this method is effective

Free writing is effective because it forces you to make notations of all of your passing thoughts on a topic. Many students get stuck determining what to write about because they feel as though every idea they write down has to be good. The critical and logical part of the brain stifles the creative process. By temporarily turning off that critical process, ideas can flow freely without restriction. Even unrelated thoughts can lead to topics for papers or at least become ideas related to a particular topic you can look into. Free writes are particularly helpful for students who tend to have many ideas for a paper and then forget them or dismiss them as bad as soon as they need to make an outline or write the paper.

Brainstorming and Listing

Most students are familiar with the concept of brainstorming. If you have ever sat around with your friends and tossed around ideas for what to do on a day off or where to go for lunch, you have brainstormed. Brainstorming is often done in groups, classes, or committees to come up with ideas for fundraisers, parties, or other undertakings. Brainstorming is a way to generate ideas and solve problems outside a group setting, as well. Brainstorming for a paper works the same as it does in a group setting, but in this case, you list ideas that come to mind by yourself.

Randomly generating ideas

Brainstorming is similar to free writing in many ways. Ideas are generated randomly but are more structured and organized than with free writing. Unlike a mind map, a brainstorm does not necessarily flow neatly from one related concept to another. This method of generating ideas is more structured than free writing and less visual than mind mapping, so analytical students who enjoy having neat lists might gravitate toward this prewriting method. Brainstorming aims to create a large list of potentially useful information by forcing you to write down topic ideas or ideas to include in a paper no matter how ridiculous or impossible they might seem.

Tip No.

17 If you are a list-maker, brainstorm as a prewriting technique.

A huge part of successful prewriting is finding a style that works for you. People who are more analytical or list-minded might have issues with the lack of formal structure in free writing and mind mapping, but making lists comes naturally.

Listing any ideas that come to mind on the topic

When brainstorming, you can use either a piece of paper or a word processor, whichever is more comfortable. Start by listing any ideas that come to mind. Do not limit these ideas to ones that are realistic or helpful. Because this type of brainstorming is done alone, there is no need to worry about whether any ideas that come to mind are good; just write each topic or idea as it comes to you. Even if an idea is too broad or seems ridiculous, it might lead to a more useful idea later. While making this list, leave some space between each idea you write down so you can return to it and add additional thoughts that come to mind as you go along. This should not turn into an outline, but for students who like to keep their lists neat and organized, having related subpoints on this list might be helpful. Additionally, once you do hit on an idea that works, you can start a new brainstorm of additional ideas to research or include in your paper.

The following is a sample brainstorming list.

<u>**Ancient History Paper**</u>

- Greek mythology
  - Athena
  - Math and architecture

- Egyptian history
  - Mummies and burial practices
  - Pyramids and architecture
  - Hieroglyphs

- Ottoman empire

- Roman invasion
  - Christianity and religion's part

Why These Techniques Work

The one thing each of these techniques has in common is the lack of emphasis on high quality and mechanics that will become more important later in the writing process. Even more structured methods, such as mind mapping or brainstorming, allow students to write down ideas without second-guessing themselves or feeling intimidated by formal structure. By feeling free to write about anything — even how annoying research papers are — your ideas will flow naturally from one to the next. Rather than allowing these passing thoughts to become distractions, write them down, which allows the mind to move past them and onto the next thought. This greases the mental wheels. Topical ideas eventually will start to flow, and you will end up with at least one, if not multiple, usable topics.

Tip No. **18 Relax. Do not stress out over prewriting.**
The more relaxed you are when you prewrite, the better the material you will end up with. Focusing on high quality and perfectionism at this stage in the process creates undo stress that will just make picking a topic and getting the paper underway more difficult.

Anything goes at this stage of the game, so have fun with it, and find what works for you. Try all of these methods, or even make up your own. As long as it gets your thoughts down on paper and helps generate some ideas, the prewrite is successful. Relax and ignore the part of the brain that wants to edit and make everything perfect right away. There will be plenty of time for that once you find the perfect topic.

CASE STUDY: IMPORTANCE OF PREWRITING

Deanna Love
Writing Fellow (Carthage)
Information Literacy Coordinator
(St. Paul)
Carthage College Writing Center
St. Paul Public Library

I have worked at the Carthage College Writing Center for the previous three years. Students using the center include freshmen in their first seminar classes and seniors working on theses in a wide range of disciplines. The center also serves students in the adult education program and the Target Language Experts, who come from a variety of countries to Carthage to earn a Master's in education while teaching introductory level language classes. During my time at the center, I earned a level three master tutor certification from the College Reading and Language Association. This certification requires a minimum of 30 hours of advanced training and 75 hours of face-to-face tutoring. I am currently working directly with the writing center director to formulate a tutor training program designed to address the developmental writing needs of students requiring remedial writing help. I will soon begin a 12-month appointment with the Rondolo Community Outreach Library in St. Paul, Minnesota, as an information literacy coordinator. I will supervise the Homework Help Center and providing tutor training emphasizing the writing needs of those learning English.

One of the biggest pieces of advice I can give is not to disregard the prewriting stage. Time spent preparing to write saves time later. It also makes the entire process of writing a paper less intimidating. It is much easier to consider writing a draft when you have concept maps, outlines, research notes, and a clear thesis statement. Be aware of how you use time, and determine the best way to divide your homework hours. If you are struggling with time management, consider visiting a learning specialist to better understand your learning style. This knowledge can help you assess the areas in your homework or writing process that might need to be modified.

Focus and organization are two key factors that help create strong papers. Students who develop a specific thesis statement and then articulate the argument they propose in an organized manner tend to be much stronger writers than those who are unable to clearly state their ideas. Take your time, and do not be discouraged. Writing is a skill like any other and requires practice. Seek advice from experienced students, writing tutors, and your professors. These resources can help you identify topics, form a thesis statement, and outline an argument.

Read the assignment. Read the assignment. Read the assignment. Often, professors will provide clues for the type, tone, and topic of a paper directly within the assignment sheet. Look for key words and concepts. Then, use those key words to begin brainstorming possible ideas. Use concept maps or Venn diagrams to start organizing those initial thoughts. Review class notes and texts. Try free writing. Take five to ten minutes to just jot down any ideas and thoughts that come to you without worrying about grammar, organization, or anything except what comes to the forefront of your mind. Take your time developing a strong, clear, and focused thesis statement. Perform any required research. Then, begin drafting your paper. When students invest more time in the prewriting process, they face fewer struggles writing a paper.

Do not be afraid to ask the librarian for assistance. They will be delighted to help. Look at the sources referenced in the initial sources you find; those references can lead you to the key documents that play a foundational role in your topic. The Internet can be a powerful research tool, but always be aware of the possible weaknesses of an Internet source. Look for articles and sites educational institutions or legitimate organizations provide. Ask your professor if you have any doubts.

If you can force yourself to stay organized while prewriting, you will find it easier to organize your information later when you need to do your citations. Citing any idea that comes from another source is essential. Please, please, please take the time to formulate citations when you initially find the information, and insert that citation into your paper immediately after using a source. Students lose so much time trying to go back at the end and remember every citation. The drastic consequences of plagiarism in a college setting include failing the assignment, failing the course, and even being expelled. Plagiarism is no joke, and it is imperative every student learn how to cite sources. If you don't know how to cite sources, seek help. Your professor, writing tutor, or librarian will teach you.

Study Guide

- Prewriting should be done to help generate ideas for a paper. It is a vital step that will save you time later.

- Prewriting is a way to narrow a broad assignment into a handful of topics that interest you.

- Three common types of prewriting are mind mapping or clustering, free writing, and brainstorming or listing.

  - Mind mapping constructs a web of interconnected ideas as they come to mind.

  - Free writing forces you to write and write without stopping until you have generated ideas for your paper.

  - Brainstorming works for people who like lists because it allows them to list any ideas that come to mind for their paper regardless of how feasible the ideas are.

- Prewriting methods can be combined or even invented, so if none of the methods discussed here are working, find what does work.

- Prewriting should be loose and less structured than normal writing, so relax, and do what comes naturally.

CHAPTER 3

Narrowing Your Focus and Developing a Thesis Statement

The biggest mistake students make when getting ready to write a research paper is choosing a topic that is too broad. Although all of ancient Egyptian history might be interesting, condensing everything there is to say about it into a short research paper is a daunting, if not impossible, task. Jumping into the paper without narrowing the focus will leave you frustrated and confused later when you pick through all the information you have and decide what to include. With a limited focus already in mind, however, choosing what information to include becomes a less worrisome and time-consuming process. The trick is knowing when you have found the right topic.

Tip No. 19 Start broad, and then whittle the topic down until it feels right.

Prewriting forces you to generate many ideas, and the ideas you get from it will likely be too big to cover properly in your research paper. Recognizing this will allow you to zoom in on the most interesting or pertinent aspects of the topic that will make for the best paper.

Finding a Broad Focus, and Narrowing it Down

Recognizing a good paper topic when you come up might not be easy. Ideally, a good paper topic should be all of the following:

- Appropriate for the scope and subject matter of the class you are writing the paper
- Something you find interesting and will enjoy researching and writing about
- Easy to find good research materials for
- Something with an argumentative aspect to it
- Not so broad that covering it would be impossible within the length of the paper
- Not so narrow that saying enough on the subject would be difficult

Understanding what a topic should cover and determining how to make the idea work as a viable research paper can be difficult. You might get lucky and hit on a topic that will require almost no additional refocusing, but you more often will need to tweak your idea slightly until it has a properly narrowed focus.

Tip No. 20 Understand few topics will be perfect.

In an ideal world, any topic you choose would be exactly the right size and have tons of available resources, but this will not always be the case. Do not give up or get discouraged if you have trouble with something about your topic or you find out later it is too broad or narrow. These are fixable issues, so there is no need to panic.

How to narrow the focus

Students who have taken to some of the prewriting techniques might find those same methods useful in narrowing the focus of their topic. *Prewriting techniques are discussed in Chapter 2.* If narrowing what to focus on seems tough, make a mind map or brainstorm some angles to approach the topic from. Another method is to conduct online searches for the topic to see what other people have said about it. Perusing the library's selection of books on your topic might give you an idea for how to approach

the subject, as well. Most school libraries have access to books and electronic databases full of articles on almost every topic. Reading a few articles on a subject can be a way to get ideas. Check the assignment parameters on the class syllabus or check with the professor to get some clues for how to narrow the focus. Bouncing ideas off friends and classmates even can be useful. Most importantly, make sure to take full advantage of all of the resources available to you. Many campuses have more resources for writing papers than students expect, so ask a librarian or professor for help if you do not know what you have at your disposal.

Litmus Test

Consider these questions as a sort of litmus test for your paper. A litmus test is used in chemistry to test the pH of a substance, but the term is also used in other situations that involve a crucial pass or fail test. Your topic does not have to pass this test with a score of 100 percent, but the better it fairs when you ask yourself these questions, the easier things will be for you later. There could be at least one category in which your topic fails. You might be required to write a paper on a classic piece of literature, such as *Hamlet*, that hundreds, if not thousands, of scholars have written about. You might have to write an argumentative research paper on a hot-button issue for a politics class. If it is part of the assignment, that is fine, but make the paper as strong as possible in every area in which you can help it. You will save yourself a headache later

Asking yourself questions will help narrow the focus or make sure you already have narrowed your focus properly. Once you have an idea or two about how you might want to tighten your research topic, use the following checklist to determine whether you are on the right track:

1. **Is this topic still too broad?** You might think you have narrowed your topic down enough, but it might still be too broad for the time and length of the project. A good way to test this is to do an online search for your refined topic and see what sort of information you get. If professionals have written volumes about your topic, it might be too broad for a five-page research paper though you might want to save it for a senior project or dissertation later. For now, pick one element of your topic to focus on, and see whether that helps.

2. **Is this topic too narrow?** In the effort to get away from being too broad, students can go too far in the other direction and wind up with topics too narrow for the scope of their papers. If you have to write a long research paper and can only find a handful of research materials that touch on your subject, you might need to expand slightly. There might also not be enough to say about your topic to fill the length the assignment requires, or it might be too in-depth for the scope of the assignment. Find a related aspect of the same topic to include in your argument or another way to expand the focus slightly. If all else fails, refocus and save the narrow topic for a short paper later.

3. **Does this topic fit the parameters of the assignment?** After prewriting, conducting the preliminary research, and getting the topic narrowed, students might lose sight of what the original assignment was. Before you commit to a topic, double-check the assignment information, and make sure your topic meets all the requirements your professor gave. If it does not, determine whether you can adjust it slightly to get all of the requirements in. Bounce ideas off classmates or meet with your professor to discuss how to make the topic work if you find yourself stuck.

4. **Is this topic argumentative?** With rare exceptions, every research paper should be argumentative in some way. Research papers are not just about compiling a bunch of research and then repeating everything you discovered about a topic. The best papers aim to convince the reader of something based on the research that has been gathered. For example, a paper might argue Paul Revere was given too much credit for his part in the Revolutionary War or noneducational TV programming is often more accurate than

educational programs. Find controversy within the topic, and craft an argument from that. If there is no way to make the topic argumentative, you might need to find a way to refocus it to find an argument.

5. **Is the topic too controversial?** Argumentative is good, but going with too controversial of a topic can be too much to handle. Certain subjects are deemed taboo or get everyone riled up when they are mentioned. If you find your topic is embroiled in too much controversy, you might need to pick and choose what you want to cover. Controversial topics can make some of the best research papers, but they need to be treated delicately. Students who are intimidated by arguments or challenges to their opinions might want to stick to safer topics.

6. **Why is this important? (Or, who cares?)** This question absolutely needs an answer. If the answer to "Who cares?" is "No one" or "I don't know," you might need to find a new topic or at the least refocus it. If the writer does not know why anyone would want to read a research paper on his or her topic, odds are good the readers will not know why the writer bothered to write it. Determine whom this topic will appeal to, and then keep that audience in mind while writing the paper.

7. **Are there enough materials available for me to research this?** Always do a preliminary check for research materials before committing to a topic. Few things are more frustrating than finding what seems to be a usable topic but then finding out after doing all the preliminary work there are not enough reliable sources on the topic to do a proper paper. Checking the library and its electronic databases is a good place to start. If you cannot find sources that

look credible while doing a quick search for a paper of average length, you might want to adjust your focus to find more sources. It is possible to do a paper without many readily available sources; it just makes the process more challenging.

8. **Is this topic fresh? Is there still something to say about it?**
    Be particularly wary of this one if the topic you have chosen turns up a ton of sources. Having enough research material available is nice and makes things easier, but if a topic has been around for a while or is a hot-button issue, finding something new and creative to say about it might be difficult. Shakespeare's *Hamlet*, gun control, and the death penalty are good examples. These topics have tons of information out there, but scholars and pundits have written so much about them it can be hard to find something new or innovative to say. If you are set on writing your paper on a topic like this, find out whether anything fresh is being written about it by looking for recently dated articles. Also, be extra careful when wording your thesis statement to make sure you are not making the same points as everyone else.

If the topic passes this checklist with or without some adjustments along the way, odds are good it is the start of a paper. It might need to undergo later revision, but for now, you are ready to start working on developing this topic into your paper's thesis statement.

Tip No. 21 **Have a backup — just in case.**
Even if you think your topic is absolutely perfect, it does not hurt to have a backup idea in mind in case you run into unforeseen trouble later and have to change. Keep a couple variations on your narrowed topic on file somewhere. Even if they do not come in handy for this paper, they might come in handy for another one later.

Developing a Thesis Statement

A thesis statement is an important part of writing a research paper, but the difference between a refined topic and a thesis statement might be unclear. The topic of a paper is what the paper hopes to cover or prove in a loosely defined sense. A thesis statement, by comparison, is a declarative statement made in the introduction of the paper that lets readers know what the paper is going to inform them about. It should serve as the framework for writing your paper from start to finish. The thesis statement is one of the most vital aspects of the paper because it is a guide for the writer and it should grab the readers and convince them the paper is worth taking the time to read. A weak thesis statement is often the sign of a weak paper, and the last thing students want is for their professors to label their writing as weak from the beginning. Even if the rest of the paper is well-written, having a weak thesis will make the paper feel unfocused or lacking.

Tip No.

22 The thesis statement is the framework, or guide, for your paper, so make sure it is as strong as possible.

For the rest of the writing process, you will be referring back to the thesis statement. It will help you write your outline, and all of your research will be done to support this thesis statement. It is the most important sentence of any paper, so give it the time and effort it deserves.

Creating the frame: Turning a topic into a thesis

By now, you should have some notes about your chosen topic and aspects within it you are thinking of covering. You might even have some backup ideas in case your focus changes during the research process. Turning  that information into a solid thesis is simple, but it can be difficult. The process is not difficult, but as with any skill, it requires practice and can take several tries to get right. Thesis statements are often intimidating to writers, but they can always be revised and likely will need to be revised slightly as you do more research. Do not let yourself get too stressed out about it at this stage. However, be sure to take the time to craft the best thesis statement you can now because it will save time and frustration throughout the process.

When beginning to craft a thesis, writers should keep a few things in mind. A solid thesis statement should meet all of the following criteria:

- It is a statement of the paper's message and purpose.
- It must be declarative.
- It has a clear direction or frame for the paper.
- It needs to have a hook to make it interesting.
- It must be clearly worded and concise.
- It must be void of weak language.

These points are a checklist to keep handy while crafting a thesis. The following section will take a more in-depth look at each of them.

For Science Students

The thesis statement is like your paper's hypothesis. It is what you hope to prove with your paper in the same way a hypothesis is what you believe you will prove with an experiment. The difference is that you do not know whether you will prove your hypothesis at the start of an experiment whereas your entire paper should be structured to support and prove your thesis. Structurally, there will be some differences, but if you can write a hypothesis, you can write a thesis statement. If you are writing about your own scientific research, your hypothesis can even be edited to become your paper's thesis statement.

Message and purpose

The thesis statement describes the point of your paper to readers. A good place to start when drafting a thesis is to ask yourself what point you want to make in the paper. This relates to the argumentative aspect. Based on the little preliminary research you have done and the knowledge you already have about your topic, you should have an idea of what you are hoping to prove, such as, "I will prove gun control laws should be more/less restrictive," or "I will show that Paul Revere did not have as large of a role in the American Revolution as people think." Although statements like these are not the best thesis statements and might not be considered thesis statements at all, with work, they can turn into good thesis statements. If this step proves difficult, conduct more research or ask yourself questions until you form a solid opinion on your topic. You might change this opinion later, but have an idea going into your paper of where it will end up and which conclusions you will draw.

Declarative statement

Once you have nailed down your paper's central point or purpose, the next step is to make sure that what you are saying about the subject is a focused declarative statement. Do not meander away from your point. State whatever you are hoping to prove with authority. This is an opinion on the topic, but by doing the research necessary to write this paper, you are becoming an authority on the topic. Act like one. Avoid using words that make it seem as though you are questioning your knowledge or authority on the subject. Phrases such as "I think" or "I feel" weaken your argument. Instead, use statements such as "This paper will." Anyone reading your paper assumes your argument is your own opinion and your statement in the paper is what you are hoping to prove. Restating this information adds extra bulk to your thesis and does not look professional. You want to be streamlined and authoritative if you want to get noticed.

Also, never use a question as part of your thesis statement. Including questions might seem to be an interesting stylistic choice or a way to draw in readers. Writers can use questions effectively, but questions more often make writers seem as though they do not know what they are trying to prove or are asking the readers for their opinion. This paper should showcase your knowledge and the research you have done. By using a question, you take the spotlight off yourself. Stating the point of the paper with absolute authority is key to writing a thesis statement that will impress professors.

A direction

Once you have a clear sense of the purpose of your paper and are sure your phrasing carries authority, give your statement more direction. Get out the notes you have taken so far, and choose a few things you know you want to include in your paper. These ideas should help form the basis for your thesis statement, so be sure to pick supporting ideas that underscore the main point and add credibility to your argument. You can always change these later, but the thesis statement should act as a frame for your paper. This means it should include information about which key points will be covered in the paper to support the main argument.

For example, a paper on enacting more restrictive gun regulations might prove it has a direction with this thesis statement: "Gun control regulations might restrict the purchase of certain weapons, but they do not do enough to keep guns out of the hands of dangerous criminals or ensure citizens who purchase guns know how to properly use them." The reader knows the paper will argue gun control regulations should be stricter. He or she also knows the author will argue more needs to be done to keep guns out of the hands of certain people and better train people who purchase guns on how to properly use them. This gives the reader clues about what to expect in the paper and gives the author a reference point to return to while writing the paper. If you get lost while writing your paper and are unsure of what to write next or where to include a piece of information, the thesis statement should serve as the road map for information and as the basis for writing an outline. *Writing an outline will be covered in Chapter 5.*

Tip No. 23 You can always change your thesis statement later.

If it helps reduce the pressure, think of the thesis statement you are crafting now as temporary. It is a placeholder for the thesis statement that will end up in your final paper. If the direction of the paper has changed once you have done more research, you can revise your thesis. In a perfect world, students would never have to revise their thesis statements, but opinions can change as they become more informed. Students might even disprove their original thesis through research.

A hook

Once you have a thesis statement containing the main point of the paper and outlining the direction in which your argument is headed, the bulk of the work is complete. These elements are the meat of a thesis statement. The rest of the work is adding the depth and finesse that get a paper noticed. Make sure the thesis statement has a hook to ensure your paper has punch or pizzazz. If the thesis statement is boring, readers will not be interested in taking the time to read

the rest of the paper. Start off with a fact or piece of information that is shocking or otherwise grabs attention. For example, rather than stating that divorces are bad for children, you might say, "When compared to children who have suffered a death in the family, children from divorced homes experience more psychological trauma and mental health issues later in life, which is why society should re-examine relationship and familial expectations." This statistic is surprising, and it grabs the reader's attention, which encourages him or her to continue reading. Topics that are already controversial or widely appealing have the intensity and interest without your extra effort, but some topics might require more time to add flair. Regardless of the topic, the thesis statement should have style and be written in your own voice.

Adding style to writing is something that students often find difficult, especially because writing with a unique voice is difficult to teach. It takes time and practice to develop a writing style. The topic you have chosen to write about is something interesting to you. Think about why you find the topic interesting, and make sure the thesis statement reflects that. Let your personality show in your writing. Reading other papers and essays will give you an idea of what makes a style unique, but be genuine, and your style will show through your words.

Tip No. 24 Be yourself.

It can be tempting to sound lofty and academic in papers, but writing in your own style will help make a paper stand out from the pile. Developing a style is a hard thing to teach, but it comes with practice. Just write what comes naturally. When you are relaxed and having fun with a project, it shows. It naturally makes the topic more interesting to readers.

Clear, concise wording

Like writing with style, writing concisely takes practice. Students often make the mistake of being verbose, or wordy, in their writing. It can be tempting to whip out the thesaurus whenever you get stuck and find a big word to add flair or use too many words to state simple ideas. Many students suffer from the misconception that more or bigger words somehow make their writing better or sound smarter. These extra or complicated words just muddy the waters and make it difficult to understand the point the author is trying to make. This is not to say students should not use their vocabularies to their advantage, but they should make sure they use these words to maximum effect. Especially never use two words when one will do in the thesis statement, and keep the wording straightforward. A good way to ensure you are doing this is to go through your thesis statement and cross out every word that is not directly contributing to the main idea of the sentence. Add back in any words that are absolutely necessary so the sentence still makes grammatical sense. This exercise will reveal places in which some excess fat can be trimmed from your wording. You need to condense the point of your paper into one to two sentences, so use the limited space you have as wisely as possible.

Pruning a Sentence

This is a writing exercise that many writing classes use to teach students how to write concisely. It is a form of extreme editing, and it is a tool to help you understand what the most important parts of a sentence are. To practice pruning a sentence, you will need to take a sentence, in this case your thesis statement, that is not as concise as you would like it. Here is a sample thesis statement from a paper about Edgar Allan Poe's *The Tell-Tale Heart*. To prune it, all the nonessential parts of the sentence have been crossed out.

> ~~Though the~~ narrator assures ~~the~~ reader
> ~~several times that he is~~ not mad
> ~~it seems as though he is~~ trying ~~to~~
> convince himself ~~of this fact, rather~~
> ~~than the reader as these instances~~
> ~~only work to further~~ illuminate
> ~~his~~ insanity.

This entire statement was pruned down to ten important words. See how much fluff there was? Once the excess has been trimmed, go back in and add words that are needed to make it a complete sentence again.

> The narrator repeatedly assures the
> reader he is not mad, but he is
> trying to convince himself of this
> as each instance further illuminates
> his insanity.

See how much shorter and more concise this sentence is? It gets the same information across in half the space.

Choosing the right words

Mark Twain once said, "The difference between the right word and the almost right word is like the difference between lightning and a lightning bug." The goal is to write a thesis statement that will impress, so choosing strong words is vital. Which is more impressive: lightning or a lightning bug? The answer is obvious, so use strong words as often as possible. The chances that you removed a lot of weak words while trimming excess words from your thesis statement are good. Always be sure to double-check for repeated words  and poor word choices before finalizing a thesis statement. Qualifying words and phrases, such as sort of, kind of, a bit, really, and very, add extra fluff without telling the reader anything useful. When qualifiers are needed to describe something, use more quantitative phrasing. For example, you might say, "60 percent of" instead of "most of." The word that is also overused. Many sentences that use the word that can be reworded so that is not included. For example, the previous sentence could read, "Many sentences can be reworded to remove the word that from them." This revision reads much more clearly.

Tip No. 25 Make yourself sound credible.
Avoid using dodgy words or vague language in your thesis. Such tricks are often used to cover up that writers do not have all the facts to back up what they are saying. You will have all the facts, and you should have nothing to hide, so write a paper that sounds like it. If you question your own credibility, other people will too. *Chapter 4 discusses credibility*.

When choosing powerful words, be aware of clichés. It can be tempting to use cute or clichéd language to spice up a paper or give it more personal flair. By nature, these statements are overused and lack creativity. If, for some reason, using clichéd language is unavoidable, put a new or creative spin on it. Still, this can make a paper seem unprofessional or cheesy, so use this approach with caution. It might be true that clichés can occasionally be used effectively, but professors might still frown upon their use, so it is best to avoid them as much as possible. Also avoid slang and informal phrasing unless it relates directly to the topic. The thesis statement and the rest of the paper should be as polished and professional as possible, so do not use language and phrasing inappropriate to an academic or professional setting.

Simple versus complex thesis statements

Most papers will only require a simple thesis statement, but longer papers, such as senior projects or graduate-level work, might require a complex thesis statement to properly convey the paper's purpose. The simplest thesis statements follow some variation of, "This is true because of these reasons" or, "Despite this opposing viewpoint, these reasons are why this is true." More complex topics might require longer thesis statements that come in two parts. The first sentence sets up the argument, and the second sentence gives the real point of the paper and the supporting reasons. Use whichever is appropriate to the situation.

Thesis Statement Examples

By now, you should have a solid understanding of what makes or breaks a thesis statement. Below, you will find nine sample thesis statements. Each has a few problems that need to be resolved. These problems are then explained, and a revised example is given for your reference.

1. **Shakespeare's *Romeo and Juliet* is odd for a tragedy.**

    This is an acceptable start for a thesis statement, but it lacks specifics. Why is it odd? Where is the argument going? Although these questions might not be answered entirely in the thesis statement, they should at least be addressed.

    Revision: With the exception of the opening lines, the beginning of *Romeo and Juliet* is set up using the comedic conventions of Elizabethan theater, which makes it Shakespeare's strangest tragedy.

2. **Sharks do not kill as many people as people seem to think they do, so the media-portrayed shark threat is overblown and stupid.**

    This thesis statement is far too wordy. The word "people" is repeated unnecessarily, and the phrase "overblown and stupid" lacks professionalism. There is also little specific language here to back up what this person is saying or give the paper a direction.

    Revision: Sharks pose little risk to humans and kill fewer than one person in the United States per year. Despite this, pop culture and media portrayals hype the danger unnecessarily.

3. **Current gun control laws do a lot to keep some types of weapons off the streets, but they do not do enough to keep guns away from criminals or teach consumers how to use them.**

   This thesis statement is not terrible, but it uses vague language in the beginning. It is wordier than necessary and flat. It lacks oomph or passion. Again, this thesis statement is not bad or wrong, but it is not award winning, either.

   Revision: Regulations on military-grade weapons and ammunition, for example, do help to keep dangerous weapons off the streets, but gun control regulations are still strongly lacking when it comes to keeping guns away from criminals and teaching civilians how to properly use the weapons they are able to purchase.

4. **Many of Egypt's historical artifacts are housed in London, not Cairo, like they should be.**

   This sentence lacks punch. It also does not strongly present the paper's argument. It starts to give a direction but fails to fully flesh that out. It also lacks finesse. It is still an acceptable starting point for a thesis statement, but it needs some oomph and more substance to make it sound stronger.

   Revision: To this day, England's museums house more Egyptian artifacts than the Egyptian Museum, which is located in Cairo, despite attempts to rectify this. Although delicate artifacts could be destroyed or damaged by relocating them, several other pieces should be moved back to Cairo because they are part of Egypt's rich history and many of them were obtained unethically.

5. **I believe that as long as news media remains a business, bias will remain in the media because reporters must report news that sells.**

   The phrase "I believe" automatically weakens this thesis statement. The statement does give the main point of the paper, but it is otherwise lackluster and weak. It needs a stronger direction because it does not set up a strong frame for this paper. The reader is not sure what exactly will be covered, and the author might get lost while writing without that solid framework.

   Revision: Journalists have an ethical responsibility to report all news accurately and without bias, but the media is a business and must report news that makes money. Donations from and affiliations with corporations that keep media companies afloat perpetuate bias and unethical reporting.

6. **Despite not being formally recognized by most literary scholars as part of the canon, J.R.R. Tolkien is one of the most influential authors of the last century.**

   This is a good example. It states an argument, and the fact that Tolkien fantasy has had a resurgence in popularity recently adds an element of interest to it. It still could frame the argument better, however.

   Revision: J.R.R. Tolkien's works are timeless and inspiring and have contributed to the literary community, so scholars should recognize the author as part of the literary canon.

7. **The portrayal of criminologists on television is bad for the criminal justice field because it floods the field with students and job seekers who don't really understand the profession.**

The language here is informal. The use of a contraction is frowned upon, if not forbidden, in almost every academic setting. The rest of the thesis is not horrible, but the use of ambiguous words, such as "bad," does not give it the right authoritative tone.

Revision: Although the glamorous portrayal of criminal justice work in pop culture might increase the number of students studying this important field, it ultimately hurts the profession by flooding the job market with misinformed individuals who do their jobs incorrectly and do not enjoy the work.

8. **Despite the evolution of higher-resolution graphics and more lifelike controls in recent years, video game brutality does not consequentially impact the cognitive development or behavioral tendencies of today's progeny.**

This is what happens when you try to add style and flair by going through a thesaurus and replacing words with bigger ones that seem to be more intelligent. Doing this sparingly to come up with more potent words is acceptable, but it just makes your writing more difficult to understand when overdone. Also, starting with "despite" makes it seem as though the author is hoping better graphics will negatively affect children, which is opposite of what is being argued.

Revision: No significant evidence proves video game violence has a negative impact on a child's cognitive or behavioral development even with the advent of higher-resolution graphics and more lifelike controls.

9. **Webcomics are totally increasing in popularity, gaining a lot of cred in the industry. They are starting to overtake print comics and might soon give them the boot entirely.**

This example takes using informal language and slang to the extreme. Trying to add interest by using phrasing such as "cred" and "the boot" might work with your friends, but in a professional academic setting, it comes off as juvenile and will give most professors the wrong impression. If this were a paper about the use of slang in modern culture, it might be more appropriate, but in this example, your thesis statement could be filled with words that would better define the direction of the paper and give it more substance.

Revision: Due to the popularity of the Internet, Webcomics are starting to overtake print comics in popularity and will play a key role in the future of the comic industry despite critics dismissing them as a lower art form.

Tip No. 26 **Make your point, and then say why.**
The most vital components of a thesis statement are the what and the why. Any thesis statement should explain which point the paper is making and then give a basic reason, or several reasons, why this argument is valid. As long as you make a solid point and use your support to give your paper direction, you will be well on your way to a successful thesis statement. If there is one part of a thesis statement that you absolutely cannot get wrong, this is it.

CASE STUDY: THESIS STATEMENTS AND GREAT PAPERS

Maria Carrig
Associate Professor of English and Theater
Carthage College

I have been a college professor of English since 1994. I have graded countless papers and taught the writing and editing of papers.

A great paper has several virtues. First, it shows an understanding that ideas matter. Anything worth writing about should matter to the writer and to the audience of the writer, including fellow students, fellow writers, and the world. It has a sense of drama. The writer might be analyzing a text, exploring an issue, or proving a point. The great paper does this successfully and gives the reader an answer to the question, "So what?" Second, a great paper, however creative and offbeat, shows a rational, logical mind at work. The reader can follow and be convinced by the paper's movement from one idea to the next. Third, a great paper has that elusive quality called voice: it shows originality of thought and expression and careful, elegant, and creative choices of words.

Think of your finished product in the way you think of going on a date: Appearances matter. You want your reader, your date, to see you have taken the time to make a good impression because you respect yourself and you respect him or her.

Spend an adequate amount of time working on your thesis statement. Ideally, a thesis statement answers a difficult or complex question or problem that matters to readers within the framework the writer sets up. Clarity is important, but don't oversimplify because you might prove the obvious or argue something absurd.

I had problems with writer's block and procrastination throughout my career as a student and still do. Overcoming these involves breaking the process into manageable parts: free writing; keeping the words flowing even when ideas aren't coming; showing my work to others at every stage; and most importantly, creating the time to write and not allowing myself to be distracted when it is my writing time.

Although writing well involves mechanical elements, becoming a writer is a lot less quantifiable than mastering rules. Good writers read frequently and, consciously or unconsciously, imitate the writers they like. Good writers write frequently, including informal, private writing such as journaling; collecting quotes, ideas, and fragments; and writing poetry. Good writers share their writing and know writing is like a conversation with friends, with other writers and texts, with oneself. It is never finished, and it is never perfect, but that is the beauty of it.

Study Guide

- Narrowing the focus properly is important. Make sure you consider the type and length of the paper you are writing before you begin narrowing the focus.

- Once you have an idea for a narrowed focus, run it through the checklist on page 48 to make sure it passes.

- Consider keeping a backup topic or two in mind in case you run into problems later during the writing process and need to shift directions.

- Once you have a narrowed topic, the next step is to construct a thesis statement. This thesis statement is the most important sentence in the entire research paper, and it will be a road map for your research and planning.

- A good thesis statement should:

    - State the paper's message and purpose.
    - Be declarative.
    - Offer a clear direction or frame for the paper.
    - Have a hook to make it interesting.
    - Use clear, concise wording.
    - Avoid weak language.

- Read your thesis statement several times, or have friends or tutors check it for weak spots to be sure it is as strong as it can be.

- You are still early in the writing process, and you can always change or alter your thesis to better fit the research you do later.

CHAPTER 4

Research

Once you have a narrow topic and a good idea where you want to go with it, start researching

the topic. The research collected during this stage will provide the backbone for your paper. Researching provides its own challenges, however, and many students fall into common traps without even realizing it. This chapter will help you avoid some of these common pitfalls and teach you how to find and evaluate sources of information.

CASE STUDY: RESEARCHING LIKE A PROFESSIONAL

Karl R. Olson
Curriculum Management Specialist
Herzing University

CLASSIFIED CASE STUDIES
TM
directly from the experts

Undergraduate degrees in politics and government and in international relations gave me plenty of opportunity to work on my paper-writing skills. Before I was finished, I knew several different methods to present the information the instructor wanted, defend my opinion, and use a paper as an exploration of idea that allowed the writing of the paper to be a learning tool and not just an assessment of learning.

However, a graduate program in information systems management and a graduate certificate program in project management required a different style than I was used to. Papers had to contain a much more persuasive element. It was not enough to just tell what I thought and back it up with references that agreed or supported me. I had to sell my ideas by giving the what, why, how, where and when and also include analysis of costs, risks, and benefits. Papers, though not the norm, had to be, or appear to be, evidence-based.

My work experience has included teaching college courses, teaching graduate-level adjunct faculty, and developing college curricula with subject matter experts who might not have formal education training. I often have used papers to assess aptitude before engaging in a training regime or project, and I often have used papers to assess learning during and at the end of training.

A great paper reminds me of how exciting it is to learn. Most people can pound out a paper and regurgitate the information from a text or lecture, and these are painful and repetitive to read. Many people can write an essay, to whichever length you assign, telling you how many ways their opinion is right and why you must agree with them. Reading these papers often feels like listening to a salesperson sell something you would never buy. The best papers don't preach at you or just fulfill requirements.

They start a conversation with the reader and walk him or her through what it was like to be ignorant on a subject and how careful you had to be learning the information and picking, screening, and verifying sources. Great papers walk you through the missteps of learning and accept the mistakes as part of the learning process. In the end, they do not leave you feeling as though someone was telling you what you wanted to hear or someone was selling you on an idea. They leave you feeling as though you were having a rational conversation. You don't have to agree with a great paper to appreciate it; you know a rational person could agree with the argument even if you, as the grader, do not.

Write humbly. Never use Wiki. Find sources your instructor did not recommend. Find someone to review it, and make the suggested changes before submitting the paper. Many modern students have never been taught how to research. Research is not a Google search. Many universities offer classes or assistance in how to research. Once enough research has been started, be prepared to plan. A research paper is not a stream of consciousness, and you have to think about the order and flow of your presentation and arguments. Start early, and make enough time to complete the paper.

I always suggest taking one piece of paper and writing down the subject, the needed resources, and a brief, basic idea of the order of the paper. Allow yourself to be flexible; the research you do might change your opinions or idea of what is most important as the paper progresses.

Start with peer-reviewed journals. Research the authors of relevant information. Check their cited sources and their past writings. Be aware of the date of publication, and be aware new research might have contradicted your original sources. Always look for the people who most credibly argue against your original sources. Their cited references will be a wealth of possibilities, and the argument against your original source will help you identify possible biases your source had.

The only changes between now and when the Internet was not available are information is easier to get and credibility takes more work to verify. The standards remain exactly the same. Peer-reviewed information is much more valuable than journals or blogs. The researcher must be aware of who the intended audience of the information is, what the sources are, and whether there was any bias or agenda involved in the publication of material.

Find and use an organizational style that works for you, not just one you can claim works for you. Many people get frustrated or feel self-conscious about not having a traditional organizational style and never let themselves find the style that works best for them. You can organize by subject, date published, author, or even by common references cited. The test is whether you can follow and visually demonstrate an argument through your own organizational structure. If you can do it at your desk, you can do it in the paper.

A research paper is intimidating. Think of it in smaller pieces: outline writing, initial research, revision, more research, rough draft, more research, more drafts, polishing, citation page, and editing. Make sure you plan enough time for each stage; time management is easier for smaller stages.

I learned every pieced of this advice the hard way.

Finding Credible Sources

While working on a research paper, you will likely hear about making sure your sources are credible. On the surface, this sounds like an obvious and easy piece of advice to follow, but in practice, it can be  much more difficult. A source's credibility is, in essence, how trustworthy its information is. Many writers tend to believe all information in print is true. In reality, voicing an opinion or presenting false information as fact without any credentials or proof is easy for anyone, especially online. Often, sources can appear credible even when they are not, so students must be wary.

Tip No. 27 Be a skeptical researcher.
Just because something is presented as fact does not mean it is. Just because something is written in a book, article, or other type of source does not make it entirely accurate or even true. It can seem paranoid to research this way, but you will end up with higher-quality sources if you question everything and double-check your facts.

Examining source credentials and affiliations

Always research the background of any source you are considering using for your paper. Some sources will be obviously untrustworthy, but many will be presented as legitimate or seem to have credentials when they do not. The following are some points to consider when evaluating the credibility of a source:

- **What are the author's credentials?** Do not be fooled by fancy titles or degrees when reading an author's pedigree. Make sure the credentials they list are pertinent. Having a degree does not make someone an expert in every field, so be sure the author of any source is qualified to speak about it with authority because they have personal experiences or academic qualifications.

- **Which associations or affiliations does the author or publisher have?** Associating with certain special interest groups or specific points of view can lead to bias in the author or publisher. Authors or publishers who are associated with questionable practices or activities also might not be credible. Having an author or publisher associated with a specific bias does not automatically make a potential resource a bad source, but be aware of the slant of the information before using it.

- **Does the source have any noticeable bias?** How to specifically look for signs of bias will be discussed later in this chapter, but the signs can be obvious. Finding unbiased sources is best, but finding a truly unbiased source is nearly impossible in many cases. Heavily biased sources can be used effectively with some topics, but they should otherwise be avoided. Understanding the side an article is taking will allow you to question the information being presented and make sure it is factual and usable in your own research.

- **Does the author cite any sources? Are these sources credible?** Unless the author of the source was an eyewitness to an event or is analyzing data from personal experiments, his or her information came from somewhere. Beware of anonymous sources or authors who do not list where information comes from. This makes it hard to check the facts of any claims made in an article. When authors do list sources, always review them and make sure the sources stand up to scrutiny.

- **Is the source outdated?** Due to the rapid speed at which technology moves, information goes out-of-date quickly. With some topics, such as historical events, having information written a long time ago is not an issue and might even be helpful because it was written when the event you are writing about happened. In most cases, though, check the dates on any sources you are considering, and make sure they are not so old they no longer are relevant or applicable.

- **Is the source incomplete or abridged?** Some sources might not seem to be biased until you realize they are missing information. They might have taken information out of context and used it to support an argument or edited it in other ways. Some sources might be excerpts from a larger source. This can cause you to misunderstand what the source is about and use the information in it improperly or out of context.

- **Which endorsements or reviews has the source gotten?**
Book sources will often have reviews printed on them, so check
whether any reputable people have given it an endorsement.
Online retailers of books will have reviews as well, so check to see
what people are saying about sources. You can find reviews of larger
reputable websites. Some smaller sources, such as journal articles,
might not have reviews readily available, but reputable authors
will have a large body of work. Find out whether the author
has any endorsements or has written anything else that received
positive reviews.

- **Is the publisher of the source reputable?** Large publishers
or reputable magazines and journals will thoroughly check the
facts of the information they are distributing, so using sources
from well-known publishers is safe. Some publishers might have
a reputation for printing anything, so checking the facts falls to
the consumer. On the flip side, some publishers, such as those
who put out tabloid papers, might have a reputation for printing
false information. Use information from publishers with a negative
reputation with caution.

- **Does the source use loaded or vague terms to support
itself?** We discussed the importance of being specific when crafting
a thesis statement. The same rule applies when choosing sources.
Beware of sources that use vague terms, such as "recent studies
show" or "many people believe," without giving any citations to
back up these claims. Some sources also will use buzzwords to play
on the emotions of readers. Both of these traits are red flags and

should make you at least check the information. However, you might need to disregard it entirely.

- **Does the author or publisher of the source have an ulterior motive or agenda?** This partially relates to the second bullet in this list. Who or what the author or publisher is affiliated with might color the information presented. If the author or publisher is pushing a product, for example, they likely have an ulterior motive and might slant the information. Authors or publishers affiliated with politics, government, or special interest groups run into the same issue.

Evaluating for areas of bias

All sources that are not lists of data or statistics will be biased in some respects. As much as authors try to be fair and unbiased, partiality still creeps in. Every person has a slightly different perspective on life and events, and that perspective will color the way an author presents information. In some cases, the bias might be so minor it is unnoticeable, but it might be the predominant message of the text in other cases and prevent the author from presenting information accurately. Just because a source is biased does not mean it is unusable. Even biased sources can be beneficial. For example, if you are writing a paper about objectivity in the media, finding biased news articles might help support your argument. Telling the different between useful bias and bias that will harm your paper is a crucial part of evaluating sources.

The following is a list of questions to consider when evaluating a source for biases:

■ **Is the source a primary or a secondary source?** If a primary source is biased, it is less of a hindrance than a biased secondary source. Biased firsthand accounts are generally still usable, and little can be done about bias in this case unless multiple firsthand accounts exist. *For more information on primary and secondary sources, reference the respective sidebars on page 84.*

■ **Does the author admit to a bias or a particular lens?** An author might admit a bias in a source. A literary critic who admits to using a particular critical lens is admitting a bias. As long as you recognize this bias and it supports what you are saying without skewing facts, the source is still useful. Biased information can also highlight parts of an argument that you disagree with and are refuting in your paper. Pointing out the bias of a source that says the opposite of what you believe can be a persuasive tool. You can also present an opinion from a different lens and then explain why you do not agree based on your research.

■ **Does the bias help support my paper?** As mentioned above, some biases, such as critical lenses, can be beneficial to research. As long as the information in the source can be verified in other sources as well, using a source like this is acceptable.

■ **Is the source purposely misleading?** Even if the bias of a source supports what you are saying, avoid sources that are purposely vague, misleading, or incomplete to paint a particular picture. Even if the part of the article you use is factual, the source will make the research seem sloppy.

- **Is the bias so overt it calls the credibility of the source into question?** Even if the facts in a source are correct and verifiable, a source that is too biased will reflect poorly on your paper. Professors might question the credibility of the source and of your own work by proxy.

Tip No. **28** Learn the difference between acceptable and unacceptable bias.

Everyone has biases, but there are differences between biases just as there is a difference between people who are so prejudiced they let their bias color their entire views of the world and people who have opinions or preferences. When the bias is mild, it can help support your theory. When it is strong, the information can be skewed. Unless you are writing a paper about bias, avoid the strongly biased sources.

Always use your best judgment when evaluating for bias. Every rule has exceptions, but you always want to use the best sources possible in your research paper. The quality of sources will affect the quality of your finished product. Showing you know how to find and use good, credible sources will also impress professors. If a source seems fishy or your gut tells you it might not be the best source you can find, keep looking until you find a better one.

Common Unreliable Sources

Here is a quick cheat sheet to use when trying to spot unreliable sources. Avoid or be highly skeptical of the following:

- Wiki sites: Wikipedia is not the only user-created encyclopedia. They come on a variety of topics. If the word wiki appears anywhere in the link or the title, avoid it.

- Personal websites: These are almost always biased, so unless it is the personal website of a scholar on your topic, be suspicious.

- Parody sites: Several parody news sites have cropped up and can look exactly like real news websites. The Onion (**www.theonion.com**) is an example of this. It seems obvious, but a surprising number of students find parody articles and mistake them for real news.

- Fictionalizations/Dramatizations: Look out for disclaimers such as "based on a true story" or "dramatization" because these reports on events often will take liberties with the truth. This applies online and in print.

Other things to consider

Beyond just evaluating for bias and credibility, consider a few other things while researching and selecting sources. Consider which types of sources will be most useful to your research, and start there. Depending on the requirements your professor places upon you and the type of paper you are writing, you might need a certain number of primary or secondary sources as part of your research. *For more information on primary versus secondary sources, see the respective sidebars on page 84.* Depending on your  topic, you might also have an idea of whether you will need more of a particular type of source. There might be a wide range of books or journal articles on your topic, or you might know you will need pictures or charts. If this is the case, start your search there, and then branch out.

Do not forget to think about the appropriateness of a particular source for your paper. A children's book about chemistry might be a useful source for a paper about teaching elementary education, but it would be inappropriate for a college-level science paper. Some classes and topics might require more formal sources whereas some professors might be comfortable allowing you to use blogs and comic strips as part of your research. On the opposite end of the spectrum, sources that are too technical might be inappropriate. Some sources might be above the level of research expected for the project you are working on, which can be just as bad as using sources that are too simplistic. If there is so much jargon in the paper you do not fully comprehend every aspect of the source, you might misuse it. Make sure every source you use is the perfect fit for the type of paper you are writing.

> ## Tip No. 29 Understand primary and secondary sources and when to use them.
>
> Some topics might use mostly primary sources, such as topics comparing pieces of literature or covering an event in history that has several firsthand accounts available. However, secondary sources are far more common. Think about the topic, decide whether primary sources will be useful or necessary, and plan your research accordingly.

Finally, be sure to ask for help while searching for the best sources. Professors are well-versed in every aspect of the subjects they teach. Most of them will offer advice and even give names or locations of good sources to use. Librarians are also helpful for students doing research. They help locate books on your topic and are also familiar with online databases, periodicals, and any other potential sources the library has access to. Campus librarians especially are accustomed to helping students with research projects and might even be familiar with your class or professor. Other students can also help, so do not be afraid to ask your friends or classmates for assistance. You might find you know people who have already taken the class you are in right now or have done research on your topic for a different class. They might have ideas for where to find sources.

Primary Sources

Primary sources are firsthand accounts of information without additional interpretation. Primary sources are often, but not always, less biased than secondary sources because they contain raw facts without another researcher's view coloring them. This does not necessarily make them better — just different. Depending on the topic, primary sources might be difficult to come by. Some examples of primary sources are:

- Raw research data from experiments
- Original works of fiction
- Statistics
- Recordings or transcriptions
- Letters and correspondences
- Diaries and journals
- Photographs or other images
- Eyewitness accounts
- Government records

Secondary Sources

Secondary sources are the result of analyzing primary sources and other secondary sources or are sources people without firsthand experience wrote. In these sources, other researchers analyze data gathered and draw conclusions based on their interpretations of that data. These interpretations will be slanted based on the viewpoint of the individual researcher though some will be more biased than others. This does not make them worse than primary sources, and this bias occasionally can help prove a point rather than make researching more difficult. However, be aware of biases in any sources. Some examples of secondary sources are:

- Biographies
- Critical reviews
- Reviews or analysis of scientific studies
- Journal articles
- Encyclopedias
- Textbooks
- Most books and news articles

Using the Library

The library is an excellent starting place for any research project. Many students underestimate how useful libraries are, especially with a new generation of students entering college who are more familiar with using the Internet to find the answers to most of their questions. There is a time and a place for Internet research, but most professors require students to use at least some book references as a part of their research. Become familiar with your campus or local library and all that it has to offer. Most libraries house thousands of books on hundreds, if not thousands, of topics and have periodicals, journals, and online information databases. All these are indispensable while doing research. Libraries are safe places to start researching because they tend to have large quantities of quality, unbiased sources. But do not assume just because you found a source in a library it is excellent. Always evaluate sources using the tips discussed earlier in this chapter.

Tip No. **30** **Befriend your librarian.**
Librarians are extremely useful partners to have while doing research. Most of them know the libraries they work in inside and out, and they might even have suggestions for sources to look into. Professors and students are helpful, too, but librarians spend the most time using the sources you are interested in, so do not dismiss how useful they can be.

Using books, references, and periodicals

Each library is a different, but most libraries have shelves full of hard copies of books and reference books, and many libraries also have hard copies of periodicals. Looking at all the resources available can be intimidating, but finding the materials you need has never been easier. Computers have made messy card catalogs a thing of the past. Your library likely has several computers set up to allow you to search for books by title, author, and keyword. There are also plenty of librarians and library assistants to help you search and locate materials if you are having trouble locating a particular section.

Unless you already know a few titles you want to include in your research, starting off with a keyword search is generally the best way to find information quickly. Search several different words or phrases related to your subject and see what pops up. Write down the names and locations within the library of any books that look promising. Most digital catalogs include summaries, publication dates, and many other useful facts about the books listed in your search results, so pay attention to these. Many catalogs also list the keywords associated with each of their books, so if you find a book that sounds as though it will be useful, see which other keywords are associated with it and search these for additional books. You might also want to check whether the same author has published any other books on the same subject. It is likely you will find more books dealing with your broad topic, rather than your narrow topic, so keep this in mind. Many books might only have a chapter or two that pertain directly to what you are researching. This is to be expected, but always choose the books from your search that have the most useful information related directly to your narrow topic.

In addition to regular books, most libraries have a vast section of reference books, such as encyclopedias. For long papers or in-depth research papers, these types of sources are too broad to be useful. An encyclopedia will give a quick overview of your subject and any related subjects you want to better acquaint yourself with. Doing this can help you come up with additional keywords to include in your search for subject-specific materials. Depending on your subject, you might also find a reference book, or several, specific to your topic. An example of this might be an encyclopedia of plants or a dictionary of scientific terms. References like these can be useful to have on hand while doing research so you can look up any unfamiliar terms or jargon in the other sources you find.

Most libraries also subscribe to a list of periodicals, such as newspapers and scholarly journals. These are wonderful resources for research because they might have articles that deal explicitly with your topic. Books could cover a broader range of information you will have to pick through. Periodicals are searchable and included in the catalog. To save yourself the trouble of searching through piles of magazines and journals, ask a librarian whether he or she has an indexed archive of the library's periodicals or a way to search them. If you tell the librarian your research topic, he or she will likely be able to point you toward a few journals or magazines that deal with your topic.

Periodicals

A periodical is any publication that comes out on a regular schedule. Newspapers, magazines, and journals are all examples of periodicals. The short articles found in periodicals are likely to cover smaller topics than books, so the chances of finding articles specifically about your topic are good. Many periodicals are making the switch to online formats, however, and many libraries have switched periodical archives for online databases. The information you will find will be similar; the format is just different

If the library does not have a way to search its periodicals by subject or keyword, many publications have websites that allow you to search their archives. Once you know which issues of a periodical have articles pertaining to your topic, you can find out whether your library still has a copy on file. Because indexing periodicals can be such a time-consuming process, many libraries have stopped keeping archived periodicals or have limited how far back their archives go. If you are having trouble finding articles pertaining to your topic or your library does not have a large collection of periodicals, do not worry. Many libraries have started to replace their periodical selection with online databases because they are easier to keep updated and to search and include a much larger quantity of information.

31 With research, start narrow and then expand.

When researching, take the opposite approach suggested for picking a topic. When picking a topic, you start broad with the prewrite and then work down to a narrow topic. To find the most applicable information possible during research, start your search with as narrow parameters as possible. Use specific keywords and criteria. Expand the search as needed to turn up more information, but the more specific you stay to the topic, the more appropriate information you are likely to find.

Using Online Library Databases

Online library databases are probably one of the best sources of articles from scholarly journals and periodicals to which you will have access. Most colleges pay a fee to subscribe to several databases, and some even provide login information so you can access them from home or school. Searching a database is similar to searching the Internet for information, but the hits returned in a search will be articles published in journals or elsewhere. You might find excerpts from books and other sources on these databases. Several types of online databases exist that cover a wide variety of subjects, so no matter which topic you are researching, you will likely find useful information.

Online Academic Databases

Academic databases are different from generic search engines. Schools, libraries, and other organizations generally pay a fee to subscribe to these databases, which contain articles from academic journals, archives, periodicals, and other sources. They save time because they contain more usable information than generic search engines and you do not have to sift through commercial websites when using a database.

How to select and search online databases

Your library will likely have information posted about how to access the online databases to which they subscribe. There might be printed instructions available or a page on the library's website with  information. If you are having trouble locating this information, ask a librarian for information about the online databases. In most cases, there will be a way to access the list of databases from a computer in the library, and each database the library subscribes to will have a small blurb about which sorts of information it covers. Pay attention to these snippets so you do not waste time on a scientific journal database if you are doing an art history paper.

Tip No. 32 Research which sorts of databases are available.

Search around, and find out which databases you have access to through your school and local library. Also, find out whether there are databases that they do not subscribe to that might be useful. Free databases could be available online. Determine whether you can find somewhere local that has access to any databases your campus or local library does not.

There are databases covering topics from art and literature to science and technology. Some cover only scholarly journals and others cover magazines and newspapers. There are also more generic ones that do not cover specific topics. To make the best use of these databases, consider following these steps during your search:

1. **Find databases pertaining specifically to your topic, if possible.** Check the brief overview of the databases you have access to, or ask a librarian or your professor for recommendations. For example, if you are doing a science paper, there will likely be at least one scientific database. There might even be a more specific database available, such as one pertaining specifically to medical research, which could be helpful for a biology paper about cancer.

2. **Set up the search parameters within the database to be as narrow as possible.** To get the most pertinent information, determine which options are available to narrow your search. Often, you can narrow your search to only include articles within a specific date range or uncheck certain types of journals and magazines that might be included in the database but have nothing to do with your topic. Also, use the most specific keywords possible when starting a search.

3. **Slowly expand your search to get additional results.** Your specific search will return few results. This is good because these results will be easier to sift through and will be current and applicable. If you do not get enough sources, slowly start to expand your date range, expand the types of journals you are searching, and use broader keywords to get more results.

4. **Move to the next database or a more general database if needed.** Once you have thoroughly searched one database, move to another to find more or better results. Some databases that cover the same topics might return some of the same results, but you might find you prefer the search system of one over another or the databases cover radically different journals and archives. You can move to a more general database, as well, to determine whether that returns better results.

Another thing to consider while searching databases, or any scholarly publication, is the difference between peer-reviewed articles and other scholarly journals. You might notice some articles are marked as peer-reviewed or some databases allow you to search for only peer-reviewed articles. Peer-reviewed articles were written by an expert in a particular field and then reviewed by other experts, or peers, for quality before publication. Peer-reviewed journals, sometimes referred to as refereed journals, will only publish articles that pass the review stage. Articles from these sources are especially useful because they can save you from checking whether other experts in the field approve of the information in the article. Scholarly articles that are not peer-reviewed are still fine as sources, but spend time evaluating the quality and bias of the article. If it is not clear whether the article was peer-reviewed, research the publication the database got it from and determine whether it is a peer-reviewed publication.

Tip No. **33** Print your articles from online sources.
Whether you find them on a database or elsewhere on the web, *always* print any articles you find and are planning to use as research. This will make them easier to annotate and ensure you have all the information needed to cite the source. It will also make it easier for you to find the source again. You might want to consider bookmarking any online sources in your Web browser for later reference as well.

Using the Internet

In addition to using the library for research, the Internet is a useful — and sometimes terrible — additional tool to have at your disposal. The sheer volume of information available at the click of a button makes the Internet valuable in any research project. Most modern college students also grew up using the Internet and turn to it to answer most of their questions, so using the Internet for research is almost second nature. The amount of information out there can be more of a hindrance than a help when students are forced to pick through thousands, or even millions, of hits for useful information. The fact the Internet also makes it easy to anonymously publish nearly any sort of information without any filter also brings the credibility of some Internet resources into question.

Types of websites

There are several types of websites on the Internet, and generally, the easiest way to distinguish them is by their domain name extension, or the letters after the dot at the end of a Web address. Here is a quick rundown on some of the most common extensions and what they mean:

- **.com:** The "com" stands for commercial. This extension is most commonly used for businesses or groups with a commercial interest.

- **.net:** This is short for network. It was originally meant to be used by information networks, or groups involved in information technology. Many people use it as an alternative to .com.

- **.org:** Short for organization, this extension was intended for noncommercial groups not fitting any of the other tags, but it is often used for personal websites and nonprofit organizations, among others.

- **.edu:** Short for educational, this extension generally denotes an elementary, secondary, or post-secondary school.

- **.gov:** Short for government, this extension is used by federal, state, and local government agencies in the United States.

Sites that end in either .edu or .gov are often, but not always, kept up-to-date and will have accurate information. Educational websites might also have links to other sources they recommend, which can be a jump-start to your online research. Sites with other endings might also have useful information, but they are often less regulated. Almost anyone can register a website, and many free website services exist that allow anyone to make a professional-looking website and publish whatever they want on it. This brings the discussion of online sources to a point that is a hot-button issue between students and professors and within the academic world.

Wikipedia

Many professors and educational institutions will specifically tell students not to use Wikipedia as a source, and for good reason. Wikipedia, for those unfamiliar, is an online user-run encyclopedia of information on a growing list of subjects and has been around for more than a decade. An Internet search of just about anything will net a result from Wikipedia on the first page. Because an anonymous online community of users runs Wikipedia, it is often criticized for containing bias, having spoof articles, and lacking citations. Anyone, from qualified experts to bored high school students, can get on and edit entries on the site. Articles on large or well-known topics are kept up-to-date and checked by moderators frequently, but things slip through the cracks. Articles can remain flagged for bias or lack of citations for months without being fixed, and people often fail to notice these tags on the articles or dismiss them.

Still, Wikipedia is the largest online encyclopedia around, and students still use it even if they do not list it as a source in their papers. Students can use Wikipedia effectively when doing research; the issue is many students do not know how to use it. References like Wikipedia are good for getting a quick and gritty overview of an unfamiliar topic. Any article on Wikipedia will not go into enough depth or provide the type of information that is useful or appropriate in a college-level research paper. Wikipedia can also be a place to start looking for sources to use in your research because any information on Wikipedia theoretically was researched by someone else and should be properly cited. If you choose to use Wikipedia, the following are a few do's and don'ts to keep in mind:

Do:

- Check to see whether the article has been flagged for any issues. These should be listed at the top of the article. Articles that have disputed neutrality or not enough citations should be treated as such.

- Check images, graphs, and other charts that might be found as part of the entry because these can be useful for gaining perspective on a research topic.

- Examine the sources listed at the bottom of the article. You might wind up using some of them as sources if they are of a high enough quality.

Don't:

- Treat Wikipedia as a scholarly source. It is not, but it might point you in the direction of other scholarly sources in the citations section at the bottom of the article.

- Quote or paraphrase Wikipedia in a paper. Plagiarized information can appear on Wikipedia, and you do not want that in your paper. As previously mentioned, many professors will not even allow Wikipedia as a source.

- Accept everything written on Wikipedia as true. Use your best judgment, and if something sounds fishy, investigate. This especially applies to any claims that do not have a citation or are marked as needing a citation.

Tip No. **34** If you choose to start at Wikipedia, do not end at Wikipedia.

Wikipedia, like any reference, is an acceptable starting point. Do not end your search for resources there though. Treat it as a jumping-off point, not an ending place for research. It can help you find sources, but this does not make it a good source itself.

Using a blog as a resource

Blogs are becoming increasingly common on the Internet. Short for Web log, blogs are written by an author, or group of authors, and generally cover a specific topic. There are blogs on just about every topic, so it is entirely

possible there is a blog out there relating to your research topic. Many blogs are strongly opinionated and can lack the professionalism expected in a scholarly source. Blogs are not appropriate for every research paper and should probably be avoided in many cases. In some papers on contemporary or Internet-related topics, it might be appropriate to use a blog, especially now that many famous politicians and media personalities are blogging. As with any source, be sure to check the author's credentials, evaluate the blog for bias, and use common sense. Also, be aware of any affiliations the blog might have. Blogs also tend to be opinionated, so double- and triple-check all facts and figures presented to make sure you are not using skewed information in your paper as fact.

Blogs and Social Networking

Today, almost everyone has a blog and subscribes to several social networking websites. News organizations ask watchers to follow them on Facebook and Twitter. Blogs toe the line of acceptable resources, and anything posted on a social networking site should be avoided. Even if they are associated with big names or major news corporations, using these as sources does not look professional.

Determining trustworthiness of Internet information

This chapter has already spent a lot of time on determining the credibility and quality of sources, but students must be especially wary of the credibility of online sources. Always approach online sources skeptically and check the facts of any information you choose to use from a Web source. Most websites on the Internet have not undergone the editing and fact-checking processes that most traditional publishers require, so people can make up false information and present it as fact online. These websites can even look and sound legitimate, so be cautious of and alert for anything that throws up a red flag.

The following are a few Internet-specific rules to keep in mind while evaluating potential online sources:

- **Check the authorship of online information.** With the exception of statistics pulled from government websites that might not list a specific author, you never want to use an anonymous online source. If they did not want their name associated with it, the source is probably not worth using.

- **Look for the date the website was last updated.** It can be difficult to determine how long a website has been active, and it might have been unattended for years or just contain outdated information. Oftentimes, there will be a note at the top or bottom of the page with this information, or on larger websites, it might be under an "about this page" section. There might also be a copyright date, which will also give you an idea of the age of the information.

If this information cannot be located, consider finding another source, or verify the information with other sources.

■ **Try to verify any credentials an author claims to have.** The anonymity of the Web makes it easy for people to say they have degrees and certifications that they do not. Search the author online, see if he or she has a personal website, and check for other pieces he or she might have written for reputable publishers. This can be difficult and daunting, but just keep an eye out for anything that seems suspicious, and trust your instincts. You can also run sources past tutors or professors for a second opinion if you are unsure.

■ **Check for citations when they seem necessary.** Plagiarism runs rampant on the Internet, and you will often find multiple websites with the exact same information, word-for-word, with no way of telling who the original author was. If a website does not offer any sources, be suspicious.

Use your head and your best judgment, and if something seems suspicious, it probably is.

CASE STUDY: A SCIENTIST'S PERSPECTIVE

Anit Raja Banerjee
Ph.D. Candidate / Research Associate
Yale University

I have graduated with honors with a Bachelor of Arts in religion and biology. I completed term papers for multiple classes and completed a senior thesis paper for each discipline.

Two types of term papers are frequently assigned in the biological sciences. One is the literature review; the other is the project proposal. They are considered productive assignment formats because academic scientists use both formats for specific, but frequently occurring, circumstances.

The literature review, or lit review, is a fascinating writing challenge in college. So much of college writing teaching is focused on a thesis statement, or making a specific point. This is not the case for a lit review in the biological sciences. A lit review summarizes the relevant literature to date, comments on current controversies within the field, and highlights the directions the field is or should be going in.

The project proposal differs from the typical term paper in college in that it also lacks a thesis statement. Instead, it presents a hypothesis, presents the current literature that forms the foundation of the hypothesis, and then presents a series of experiments to test the hypothesis. This is considered a useful assignment because scientific research is dependent on outside funding. Because of this, scientists must submit project proposals to grant agencies to fund their experiments. The assignment drives students to think critically within a scientific discipline and provides exposure to a format of scholarly writing that will be essential if that student is to pursue an academic career.

For the lit review, the first challenge is to avoid the temptation to plainly recount previous work. Such a production of a lit review often feels adequate to a writer in college. However, for a lit review to truly be valuable to the reader, it must provide more than a chronologically organized bibliography, which is all a plain recounting is.

Start with existing literature reviews on a subject of interest. Go through a few of them. Reading the first few papers within a field will be a challenging experience because you will find yourself looking up the definition for every tenth word you read. This is normal. Professional scientists looking to expand their research in new directions go through this as well. Drive your way through those first few reviews to familiarize yourself with the field. After familiarization, you should have more specific questions you might be interested in exploring. Then, start a more in-depth literature search. This can begin with some of the sources for the more salient pieces of information in the lit reviews you read.

Once you collated your sources, took notes, and came up with an idea, put together an outline before moving into writing out sentences. Think about the order of your topics, the points you want to make, the order in which to make them, and the sources you will be citing to make each point.

For the biological sciences, restrict your sources to peer-reviewed publications. That said, it is still your responsibility to familiarize yourself with the experiments conducted and critically analyze the results. The authors will come to specific conclusions based on the data they have presented. You are not obliged to agree with their conclusions if you find flaws in their methodology.

Google Scholar at **http://scholar.google.com** and PubMed at **www.ncbi. nlm.nih.gov/pubmed** are valuable resources. PubMed results, however, will be organized chronologically and not by relevance. Google Scholar presents results only by relevance and not chronologically. If you are looking for a specific discovery, Google Scholar is a better resource. If you are looking to ensure your knowledge on a topic is thorough, PubMed is the better resource.

Work your way through the web of sources at the end of each paper. Also, under the entry for each source in Google Scholar, there will be a link that will take you a list of papers that cited that particular work. The combination of these two ways of exploring the resource web will help your research be thorough and up-to-date.

A recent ten-page term paper I wrote for an early Ph.D.-level class included 28 sources. For this, I read more than 30 papers. I likely spent close to 50 hours reading in preparing for this. I found it helpful in undergraduate classes to block off large chunks of time, at least 4-hour blocks in my case, to get my mind into the reading process. As you read more and more, the tiny pieces reported in each source start to fall into a bigger picture. Reading multiple papers in a field back-to-back makes it easier to see the connections among them all.

Also, if your institution does not have an electronic subscription to all journals of interest, which only larger institutions maintain, you will need to interlibrary loan some of your sources. This will take time. It should be clear you will need to start well ahead of time to write even a decent paper, let alone an excellent one.

Train yourself to spend time asking, "How does that work?" There are biological phenomena that require some thinking to realize how cool they are. Ever thought about how we always have two eyes that are symmetrically placed? Ever thought about why leaves are green? Sure, the chlorophyll is green, but why is chlorophyll green? Ever wonder how you can get sick from *E. coli* even though there is already *E. coli* living in your digestive system? Ever wonder why your thumb looks so drastically different than the rest of your fingers? These are questions that don't require knowledge of science to ask but require knowledge of science to answer, and although the questions seem superficial and general, they still have levels of depth at which we don't yet know the answers. This is what science is about — figuring out how things work. And figuring out how something works starts with asking the right question.

Study Guide

- Finding credible sources is crucial to a research paper. You only want to use the best sources for any paper, so make sure to examine any source carefully.

- Do not assume information is accurate because it is in print somewhere. Double- and triple-check any source for false claims, bias, and loaded or vague words.

- Look into what other people are saying about a source or the author of the source and any organizations the author or source might be affiliated with.

- Become acquainted with your campus or local library and the people who work there. They will be able to help you find books, reference materials, periodicals, and more.

- Periodicals, magazines, and journals will have specific information on your topic, and many books will cover much broader topics with limited useful information. If the library does not have many of these on hand, check the online databases to which they subscribe.

- When searching online databases, or anywhere else, always start your search as narrow as possible, and then slowly broaden the search parameters to find more sources as needed.

- The Internet can be a source of information, but be sure to check domain extensions and the sources behind any information found online.

- Wikipedia can be a starting point for research, but approach anything on there cautiously because anyone can edit it.

- Always be wary of any online information, especially anonymous or improperly cited sources. Be suspicious — it will save you a headache later.

CHAPTER 5

Organizing and Outlining

Once the research is done, the next step is organizing the information. You now have several sources to pick through and decide how best to use. It is intimidating to look at, and it can be difficult to see how all of this information will fit together into a coherent research paper. That is where this chapter comes in. Once you have collected the information, you need to find a way to organize it. There are many options for organizing your information. This chapter will discuss a few different options, so try multiple methods to find which works best. As with prewriting, you can even make up your own organizational methods as long as they help you keep track of your sources and create an outline for your paper. An outline will save you time while writing, and if you do not keep track of your sources, doing citations and a bibliography for the paper will be a nightmare.

Organizing Information and Sources

Whether you use notecards, take notes, or use digital methods, such as spreadsheets, you will need to keep track of the information for your paper and where it is coming from. Nothing is more frustrating than having to dig through piles of information to find one or two sentences you were planning to quote in your paper because you can't remember where that information came from. To save time later, the following section describes a few different methods for organizing the quotes, paraphrases, and other information you want to reference while writing your paper.

Notecards

 Using notecards is probably the most common method of keeping track of information. Many teachers espouse their use in elementary school, so many students are comfortable using them once they reach college. Other students find them time-consuming and tedious. This is often because they do not understand how to effectively make notecards. Notecards are cheap and easy to find in most general stores. Many campus stores keep them on hand as well.

The most basic notecards will include the following:

- A quotation, paraphrase, or relevant piece of information
- The page number or general location of this information within the source
- Citation information for the source at least including the title and author

You can include more information if you desire, but always add these basics. Put the relevant information on one side of the notecard along with the page number or a description of where in the document this information is located. On the back of the card, write the title, author, or a complete citation if it helps you. *Proper citation formats will be covered in more detail in Chapter 7.*

Tip No. **35** Keep your notecards and other notes organized.

Color-coding or using other methods to keep notecards separate is a way to help keep your notes organized. Longer papers might require stacks of notecards, so finding a specific one in a pile of a hundred is time-consuming and frustrating. Also, consider investing in some rubber bands to keep notecards together so you do not lose any while shuffling papers or moving from one location to another.

When making notecards, also consider how you would like to organize the notecards themselves. Some students prefer to keep their notecards from a particular source together. For the purposes of making an outline, however, organize the notecards by subtopic. Break the supporting points you included in your thesis statement into points you wish to cover in your paper. Then, divide the notecards up by the points they best support. You might assign numbers to specific categories or maybe even use highlighters or markers to color-code the notecards so they are easy to keep separate. This will also make finding specific notecards much easier when it comes time to make an outline or write that part of the paper.

Tip No. 36 Even if you are not a note-taker, force yourself to write down some notes.

Did you know that when you write something down, your brain stores the information in a different location than when you read it? This is what makes taking notes so useful even if you do not go back over your notes later. The act of writing down information makes you more likely to remember it because you are storing it in two places in your brain. This is the natural equivalent of saving a backup copy of your work on your computer. If you want to make remembering information even easier, read your notes out loud to yourself after you have copied them down. You might feel goofy doing it, but it will further reinforce the memory.

Notecard example

Here is a sample notecard. Use this as a template for your own notecards, or design your own method.

Front:

```
Topic: Media Attention and Growth

Despite the recession, the criminal
justice field is still potentially growing,
especially in the area of forensic
science. This is largely due to public
interest and media attention due to the
popularity of TV crime dramas.

                                      pp. 3
```

Back:

```
John M. Doe. "The Rise of Forensic
     Science in Popular Culture"

   Article from Criminal Justice
   and Forensic Science Monthly
```

Notecards in the Digital Age

In the age of the Internet, many students prefer to use their computers for almost everything. Using digital means to organize information is handy because they are neat, searchable, and have copy and paste functions that make it easy to drop in quotes and notations. If paper notecards are not for you, type in a word document or spreadsheet. Spreadsheets are easy to use and organize information that can be found quickly. Make columns in the spreadsheet with the data, citation information, and the other information you choose to include. This should allow you to sort the spreadsheet by any of these columns, which makes looking for information by topic or author easy.

If you do not have Excel or another spreadsheet program, you can download a free bundle of word processing programs from Open Office at **www.openoffice.org**. Another alternative would be to use the function to create tables in your word processing program. There are also several programs available,commercially and as freeware, that are designed to help students keep track of notes. If you want to go digital but are intimidated by spreadsheets, you might want to consider researching other available programs.

Developing An Outline

By now, you should have done enough research to construct an outline for your paper. Odds are good that while you were reading through sources, making notecards or spreadsheets, or even brainstorming, you started to create an outline in your head, possibly without realizing it. Most students will stop at organizing their thoughts in their heads without committing them to paper. It is easy to scoff at outlines as a waste of time when you are on a tight deadline, but outlines are invaluable tools that are crucial to writing an impressive paper. They even turn out to be timesavers.

Tip No.

37 Find a trick to force yourself to outline, such as using a reward system.

Most students procrastinate the most on projects they are dreading or on parts of projects that give them the most trouble. This procrastination wastes precious time and can result in students skipping the outlining in an attempt to buy more time to work on the rest of the paper. Outlining will save you time later, so if you are a student who hates outlining, find something to force yourself to complete it. Give yourself a treat for completing an outline, or ban yourself from playing games or watching TV until you finish your outline. If you have friends who are also working on papers, plan an outlining party. Give yourself a reason to look forward to the writing process, and then reward yourself for a job well-done.

Why developing an outline is important

Your thesis statement is the paper's road map. Think of your research paper as a road trip. The thesis provides the direction, or final destination, and should give you an idea of which major stops you will make along the way. The outline is a complement to the thesis statement and acts like a trip's itinerary. An itinerary outlines each stop on a trip, the activities planned at that stop, and the time allotted for each location. Similarly, an outline should list each of your major points, the information to include with each point, and an idea of how much space each section of the paper will take up.

Tip No.

38 Your notecards will go hand in hand with your outline.

Outlines and notecards complement each other well. You can reference notecards by number in your outline or lay out your notecards on the floor or a large table while constructing your outline. These tools should mesh together so you never have to sit and figure out what comes next while writing your paper. If you are a visual person and you like the idea of a quotation outline, you can turn your notecards directly into an outline by marking them up and putting them in the order they will be referenced in your paper or taping them to a large board or piece of paper with notations. *Quotation outlines are discussed on page 120.*

Once you have gone to all the trouble of organizing your research materials and finding supporting information for you paper through notecards, a spreadsheet, or a different method entirely, you need to figure out how it all fits together in your paper. If you do not know where and how the information fits with your argument, having all the notes in the world will be like having disassembled puzzle pieces. Many students avoid outlines the same way they avoid prewriting, but this step in the planning process saves time and will help you avoid staring at a blank screen for hours coming up with what to write next. Outlines also are extremely helpful tools for remembering important information while writing the paper. Without an outline, students often find themselves rambling or meandering away from the point of their paper without meaning to or even realizing it. Outlines eliminate much of the guesswork from the writing process.

How to construct an outline

There are multiple strategies for constructing an outline, and they can range from loose notes or charts to rigidly detailed lists. Some types of outlines will lend themselves better to certain types of papers. A short research paper might only need a brief outline or flowchart to serve as a reminder for which order to cover key points in. Long research papers or scientific dissertations likely will require a more detailed outline to stay on track. Just as there is no wrong way to prewrite, there is no wrong way to write an outline for a paper as long as it gets the job done. Try different outlines, and see which helps you with your writing process the most. You might find one way of outlining that does the trick every time or develop multiple strategies for tackling papers on different subjects.

A good working outline will include the following information:

- Your paper's thesis statement
- Each of your paper's key points
- The order the key points will be addressed in
- References to your research and where sources will be included

Tip No.

39 An outline does not have to have a traditional format.

If you are a right-brained thinker and the thought of rigid outlines gives you a headache, consider making a flowchart instead. You can even make an idea web and then assign an order to each section of the web. Get some posterboard and tape to it your notecards divided by topic. Get a stack of sticky notes, write down the points you want to cover in your paper, and then stick them up on the wall and rearrange them until you are pleased with the order. If your outline does not have bulleted points or Roman numerals but helps you organize your paper's key points, it is still an outline.

The following sections will provide you with a more complete understanding of how to construct three different types of outlines. This is not an exhaustive list of outlining methods, and these methods can be mixed, matched, and altered to better suit your purposes. As long as it saves time and helps you write a better paper, you are doing it correctly.

Topic outline

The topic outline is what most students think of when they hear the word outline. This is considered to be the traditional outline and is simple in nature. A topic outline lists each topic without many details and includes any relevant subtopics below each topic. The following is an example of a topic outline:

Sample topic outline

```
I. Introduction

    A. Thesis Statement: Although the
       glamorous portrayal of criminal
       justice work in pop culture might
       increase the number of students
       studying this important field, it
       ultimately hurts the profession
       by flooding the job market with
       misinformed individuals who do
       their jobs incorrectly and do not
       enjoy the work.

   II. High Dropout/Failure Rates
```

    A. Spike in program applicants compared to popularity of crime dramas on TV

    B. Statistics for GPA and dropout rate

III. Flooded Job Market

    A. Shifts in competitiveness of job market

    B. Reality check for number of open positions in real life versus TV

IV. Impact on the Field

    A. Fantasy versus Reality

    B. Changes in field since surge in crime drama TV

    C. Satisfaction of graduates/workers

V. Conclusion

The thesis statement is the only complete sentence in the outline. Everything else is rough and loose. If this sample were a real outline, it would also include notations for where some of the referenced statistics are located, such as an author and page number or a notecard number. If you like this format but require more detail, you can include points under each subpoint. This type of outline is an excellent choice for people who do not like to outline because it is easy to construct and consists of a few brief notes to set up the flow of information. It can work equally well for long and short papers, and you can add as much or as little detail as you feel necessary.

40 Focus on the order, not the details.

The outlining stage, though more detail-oriented than the previous writing exercises covered in this book, is not the time and the place to get hung up on the specifics. You might not have decided yet whether to include everything you would like to say on a topic. The most important thing is finding a logical progression for your argument. The real goal is setting the order that points will be addressed in, not planning out everything said. You can always reorder if new ideas present themselves during the writing process. For now, just focus on giving yourself signposts to follow while writing.

Sentence outline

Another common type of outline is the sentence outline. A sentence outline is similar to a topic outline, but rather than roughly listing each topic without any details, you write each point and subpoint in a complete sentence. Sentence outlines require more thought than topic outlines, but they have the benefit of being more detailed. Although you will be putting more work into the outline, another benefit is the sentences you craft as part of the outline can often be copied directly into that part of the paper with or without minor edits. Here is how the same example used in the previous section would look as a sentence outline:

Sentence outline sample

I. The introduction of the paper will move from the broad ways in which the entertainment industry shapes our lives to the specific way the recent popularity of crime dramas has changed the face of criminal justice.

    A. Although the glamorous portrayal of criminal justice work in pop culture might increase the number of students studying this important field, it ultimately hurts the profession by flooding the job market with misinformed individuals who do their jobs incorrectly and do not enjoy the work.

II. During recent years, the dropout rates have risen and GPAs have suffered in secondary programs related to criminal justice.

    A. Studying criminal justice is seen as glamorous due to the romanticized portrayal of the field on television.

B. More students than ever are enrolling in these programs with little idea of what they are getting themselves into.

C. Statistics show the dropout rate has gone up during recent years as well.

III. Because of the rise in graduates with criminal justice degrees, the job market has become flooded with applicants.

A. Many of these applicants are misinformed about the field and their job responsibilities.

B. The competitive nature of the field makes landing "glamorous" and even low-level positions difficult.

IV. Despite the fact many of these shows try to check their facts, the characterization that lends to great drama does not accurately imitate the ways real police forces and crime labs are organized.

A. The influx of graduates, media attention, and Hollywood interest

in criminal justice has had an
impact on the field.

B. In some ways, much of what is seen
on TV is a fantasy that real life
will never be able to imitate
though the attention has changed
the field for the better in
other ways.

V. Greater public interest inevitably
leads to better funding and research.

A. Public attention is also bad
in many aspects because crime
dramas might lead to smarter, or
better-informed, criminals coupled
with misinformed workers.

B. Job satisfaction has also been
affected by the romanticized
version of crime drama seen
on television.

VI. The conclusion will start off with
a restated thesis and then address
the ways in which crime drama has
shaped the criminal justice field
and offer solutions for how it could
work to improve the field rather than
damage it.

Tip No. **41** Think about topic sentences while crafting a sentence outline.

When it is time to write the body of your paper, each paragraph will need to have a topic sentence. Think of the topic statement as a miniature thesis statement. This sentence should define what the paragraph will cover. If you keep this fact in mind while putting together sentences in your outline, you likely will find many of the sentences you wrote will become the topic sentences for the paragraphs in your body. If you take extra time now to make sure these sentences are well written, you will save yourself time later because you can import them directly into your paper.

Quotation outline

A quotation outline is different from the previous two outlines and is particularly useful for papers that require many sources. When the backbone of your paper will involve statistics from research or quotes from a book that need to be analyzed, it can be difficult to determine how to lead from one quote, paraphrase, or statistic to the next. Quotation outlines are like a combination of notecards and outlines. In this type of outline, you arrange quotes, statistics, and other information you will be using in your paper so they progress logically to support the paper's thesis. You can then build up information around these quotes to link them together and flow neatly with your argument. Even if you are not planning on paraphrasing the information in the quote, include it with citation information and notes on how the quote supports your argument.

Tip No. 42 Quotation outlines can include more than just quotations despite what the name might imply.

You frequently will find yourself using quotations at this stage because you have just copied quotes over from your notecards, but if you already have paraphrases or summaries in mind, you can include them in this type of outline. Tables, diagrams, and charts are fair game as well. If you are not yet certain which information you will be quoting and which you will be paraphrasing, use quotations and decide how to present the information within your paper later.

Here is a template you can follow when putting together a quote outline. This template uses a table format, but you could also use a spreadsheet, bulleted points, or a numbered outline if it made you more comfortable.

Paper Title		
Thesis statement:	Notes/ideas for introduction.	
Supporting Point No. 1:	"Quotation From Source" Citation Information	This supports this point because...
	Relevant Statistic Citation Information	This supports this point because...
Supporting Point No. 2:	"Quotation From Source" Citation Information	This supports this point because...
	Paraphrase From Source Citation Information	This supports this point because...
Supporting Point No. 3:	Paraphrase From Source Citation Information	This supports this point because...
	"Quotation From Source" Citation Information	This supports this point because...
	Paraphrase From Source Citation Information	This supports this point because...
Notes/ideas for conclusion.		

This template can be edited to suit the needs of your paper. You might have more supporting points, and the number of quotes, paraphrases, and statistics you include under each point will vary based on your paper and the sort of information you are planning on using. Change the template to suit your needs. As long as you list your points, the supporting evidence you are using, and some notes on how it supports your argument, you have succeeded in making a quotation outline.

43 Save your strongest argument for last.

Before you call your outline complete, look at the order you put your arguments in. Is your paper's final point before the conclusion a big one? If not, you might want to reconsider your order to determine whether the progression of ideas would be disrupted if you changed your strongest point to your last. Your paper should gain momentum as it goes. Starting off with your strongest point and ending with your weakest might cause your paper to fizzle. Make sure you end with a bang rather than a pop. If you absolutely cannot change the order you are addressing your points in, find extra support for your last point and strengthen it as much as possible.

Study Guide

- One you have done all your research, organizing it is vital. Good organization saves time later and raises your chances of constructing a well-written paper.

- Notecards are a way to organize your sources.

  ◆ Only put one quote, statistic, or piece of information on each card.

  ◆ Be sure to include citation information on each notecard.

  ◆ Consider color-coding, numbering, or otherwise organizing the notecards so they are easy to navigate later.

  ◆ Keep notecards in a box or bind them with a rubber band so they do not get lost.

- Computerized databases or spreadsheets can also be used to keep track of citation information for sources.

- ◆ These are useful because they are often searchable and can be organized by title, author, or whichever else works best for you.

- ◆ Quotes, statistics, and other information pulled from each source can be kept with the citation information for easy reference later.

- Constructing an outline is also vital and should not be skipped. Outlines save time later and provide a more detailed plan for writing your paper than a thesis statement alone.

- There are multiple types of outlines, but all should include:

  - ◆ Your paper's thesis statement
  - ◆ Each of your paper's key points
  - ◆ The order the key points will be addressed in
  - ◆ References to your research and where to include sources

- Topic outlines are basic and list key points without detail.

- Sentence outlines are more detailed and will explain each point and subpoint as a complete sentence.

- Quotation outlines are a way to organize information for papers that rely heavily on quoted or paraphrased reference material.

- There is no wrong way to organize information for your paper as long as it works for you, so experiment and find which works best for you and the type of paper you are writing.

CHAPTER 6

Plagiarism and Using Research in a Paper

Research papers require students to crawl through piles of potential sources to find support for their topics. Using these sources in the paper without plagiarizing them might seem like a conundrum to students who have not written many research papers. Plagiarism is a serious subject and should not be taken lightly. It is important to understand the difference between proper research and plagiarism. This chapter will explore what plagiarism is and what you can do to avoid it.

Plagiarism and its Consequences

Plagiarism is one of those words that you will hear around the academic community, particularly at the high school and college levels. Some writing-heavy classes might even require students to sign anti-plagiarism agreements or run each of their assignments through plagiarism-detecting software. Plagiarism is clearly unacceptable. This idea might seem simple enough, but it can become tricky when writing research papers. Students often do not have a clear understanding of exactly what plagiarism is, so resolving the need to use sources with the need to avoid copying the work of others can seem impossible.

What is plagiarism?

To put it simply, plagiarism is taking someone else's words, ideas, or other intellectual property and passing it off as your own. Think of it as not giving credit where credit is due. Any time you borrow, copy, reference, summarize, paraphrase, or quote the work of another, you must give the original author credit. Otherwise, you will be committing plagiarism. This can seem daunting, but as long as your sources are properly organized, it should not be a problem. This is why it is so important to organize your sources and write down page numbers, titles, and authors for later reference. You will use this information to give the original author credit in your work. As long as credit is properly given, there is no plagiarism. If you improperly give credit or forget to cite all your sources, however, you can quickly find yourself in trouble.

> Tip No. 44 **Look into plagiarism-detecting utilities.**
> Your professor might require you to run your paper through a plagiarism detector when you submit it, or he or she might run it through one after you have turned it in. As long as you have been careful about documenting and citing your sources, this should be no problem. Nonetheless, you might want to consider looking online for a free plagiarism scanner to run your paper through just to make sure nothing pops up that you might have been unaware of. These are not foolproof, but they do not take much time to run a scan, and scanning your paper will not hurt anything.

The consequences

It is easy to dismiss plagiarism as something other students do. You might think students who plagiarize are unethical delinquents who know they are breaking the rules but do it anyway. The truth is plagiarism also springs from confusion, oversight, and laziness. There are plenty of students who deliberately plagiarize and hope they will get away with it. There are just as many who do not realize the seriousness of what they are doing or even the fact they are plagiarizing. Dropping a few sentences into your paper and forgetting or losing the citation information can get you expelled. Plagiarism is theft. It is a question of ethics and legality.

Tip No. 45 When in doubt, cite it.
If you ever pause for a moment and find yourself wondering whether you need to use a citation for a piece of information or section of your paper, assume the answer is yes. The consequences are too drastic to take chances with this. Depending on the format the paper is in, the citations might seem time-consuming or make the paper look cluttered. Because citations are an integral part of research papers, professors will not see the paper as cluttered as long as citations are done properly. It is always worth the extra time, and academic writing is full of citations with rare exceptions.

Getting caught plagiarizing has serious consequences. In the best-case scenario, you might only fail the assignment or the class. Depending on your school's policies, however, you might find yourself expelled or facing legal action. The author you plagiarized from could file suit against you, and there are fines for violating copyright laws. Never assume no one will notice or that using a small idea or paraphrase without a citation is acceptable. It is not worth the consequences. If there is ever any question in your mind about whether something needs a citation, include one. It might be difficult, time-consuming, or annoying, but the hassle is better than risking your education. Because of how important this is, the rest of this chapter will be spent discussing when and how to use your source materials without plagiarizing.

Quoting versus Paraphrasing versus Summarizing

There are three ways to use your sources in your paper. Use this as a quick reference to understand the difference between quoting, paraphrasing, and summarizing and when to use each method.

- Quotations use the author's exact words as they are written in the source. All quotes should be surrounded by quotation marks so it is obvious they are quotations.

  Use quotes for particularly interesting and striking excerpts from your sources. Use a quote when you find a section that makes you think you could not have said the information better yourself.

- Paraphrases are different from quotations in that they do not use an author's exact words. You take the main ideas from a section of the author's work and putting them into your own words.

  Paraphrases are best used when you need to convey facts or details that you got from a source and the author's own wording is not particularly striking or important. This is also a good way to highlight how this information applies specifically to your main points.

- Summaries are similar to paraphrases but generally cover a broader section of the author's work. Summaries use ideas from a chapter or other large section of the source and are written in your own words.

  Summaries work best when you want to incorporate ideas from several different parts of the source into one sentence or a few sentences. Consider summaries when giving brief overviews of key facts that are needed to understand the core of your argument.

CASE STUDY: AVOIDING PLAGIARISM

Rachel Baldwin
Student
Carthage College

I have an easy time writing college papers. I tend to just sit down and write whatever comes to me. I have a harder time editing my papers because I tend to hate what I have written start to doubt myself. I am working on that and starting to get better, though, so the key is perseverance.

A great paper has no spelling or grammar errors, no informal language, no contractions, and no areas in or between paragraphs with words that do not flow together seamlessly. Always ask your professor EXACTLY what he or she does and does not want in the paper. These are small, simple things, but they make a huge difference in the end.

The most important advice I can give is to not think you can get away with plagiarism. You cannot. Most professors will scan every paper you write through a nationwide database. The database will flag anything you copy from a website, a book, a friend's paper, or even one of your own papers, and there will be consequences. Even if you are just taking work that YOU wrote for a different class, you need the professor's permission. If you do not get your professor's permission, you could be accused of plagiarizing yourself.

Quoting

Direct quotes are the safest way to use another author's material in your paper. Any time you use someone else's exact words, you are quoting them. Treat these excerpts as quotations by surrounding them with quotation marks and citing the source. Students could make the mistake of putting everything they cite into quotation marks to avoid plagiarism, but summaries and paraphrases should not have quotation marks. Make sure you do not change any of the words when presenting a quote in your paper. If you change the wording, it is not a quote, so putting it in quotation marks and treating it as the author's words is a misrepresentation. With web sources, copying and pasting the quote directly into your document often is easiest. If it is from a print source, double-check whether you typed the quote correctly.

Tip No. **46** Make sure your quotes are real quotes.

If material has quotation marks around it, readers will assume it is the author's exact words. This means you anything you quote down to the last comma should be correct. If you need to omit part of a quote because it is not relevant and if deleting that part does not alter the meaning, use ellipsis to signal you omitted something. If you must change a word or words for the quote to make sense, use brackets to show you changed these words. This might be necessary if the quote uses pronouns and you are not quoting anything that shows what or whom the pronoun is referring to.

Also use quotations in the proper context. Twisting someone else's words to fit your point is easy when you remove the context. Make sure you have a full understanding of exactly what the author means in the quotation so you do not accidentally misrepresent it. Read the quotation as a stand-alone excerpt to make sure it still retains the same meaning. If it does not, frame it properly in your paragraph by using a paraphrase to lead into the quote. The paraphrase should give the quote context so the reader understands what the quote means.

When to use a quotation

Quotes are used to showcase a pertinent thought from another author. Students often make the mistake of overusing quotes. If the author's wording is not particularly striking, a paraphrase often will work better. Use a quote when you do come across sentences that grab your attention, are well-worded, and hit on a key point in your argument. Only include the most interesting and vital pieces of information in the quotation. Students often make the mistake of quoting large sections of fluff when they only needed one small point. Quotes can be long but often will only be a couple of sentences. Quotes can even be partial sentences. When deciding to use a quote, choose sections of the author's work that add to your paper as they are written without having to edit or change any details.

Tip No.

47 Your quotes should showcase the best from the sources you selected.

Ideally, you will think all your sources are well-written, informative, and credible. *If not, you might want to refer back to Chapter 4.* Even if you believe everything in a source is extremely on-point and quotable, use quotations only for the absolute best points from a given source. After all, this is your research paper, and it should not read like a laundry list of quotations from other authors. Beginning writers often make the mistake of overusing quotations in their papers, so do not use a quote when a paraphrase will do.

Citations and quoting

Quotations are the most straightforward type of support to cite. Quotations, due to their nature, have a definitive start and end and a specific location from which they were pulled. Placing a citation at the end of the quotation is easy, and a quote often will come from a single page or possibly two. The citation, be it a parenthetical reference, footnote, or other annotation, will go directly after the terminal quotation mark. Parenthetical citations should always go before the period indicating the end of the sentence. If the quote falls in the middle of a sentence, place the citation where the quotation ends even if it is in the middle of the sentence. Seeing parenthetical citations in this manner could take some getting used to. Footnotes or endnotes are less disruptive because they only consist of a superscript number in the text of the paper, and the corresponding information follows later. *For more information on types of citations and common citation formats and specific examples, refer to Chapter 7.*

Paraphrasing

Paraphrases are an often forgotten but wonderful way of using sources in a research paper. Any time you take quotations from one of your sources and rewrite them in your own words, you are paraphrasing. Many students avoid doing this and prefer instead to use only quotations in their papers. They might forget paraphrases still need citations. Even though paraphrases are written in your own words, you are still using information and ideas another author originally wrote, and you must give them credit. Otherwise, you are still plagiarizing. Because paraphrases are written in your own words, they should not be surrounded with quotation marks, but they do still need a citation. You are borrowing ideas, but you wrote the actual wording. Use the citation to give the author credit without making it seem as though he or she wrote the words in your paper.

> **Tip No.**
> # 48 Changing one word does not make something a paraphrase.
>
> A paraphrase should convey the same meaning as the author's original statement but use completely different words. Notice that words is plural, which implies a more dramatic rewording than changing one word and calling it a paraphrase. Paraphrases allow you to reword another author's statements to add clarity and focus in on the aspects of their writing that relate most specifically to your paper's argument. This is not a blank check to rewrite the author's opinion to make it fit with your argument. Make sure your paraphrases showcase your writing ability, not your ability to use a thesaurus to vary someone else's word choice.

Paraphrasing will force you to familiarize yourself with more of the subject of the paper. When using a paraphrase, make sure you change the wording without completely changing the author's original meaning. You do not want to use quotations out of context; similarly, make sure you do not misinterpret the author's words or ideas when writing a paraphrase. It might be tempting to use a quote rather than look up the jargon an author uses in a particularly technical sentence. By using a paraphrase instead, you force yourself to come to a better understanding of the topic. This will make for a better paper because you will be writing with a better grasp of facts and more authority on the subject.

Tip No. **49** Try using paraphrases rather than quotes in your notes.

If you have a bad memory or are struggling to get your head around all the subtle points in your research paper, force yourself to paraphrase while taking notes rather than copy down information that seems important. This will force you to engage with the information and create a deeper understanding. You also will be more likely to remember the details of what you have read. Even though you are paraphrasing, make note of where the paraphrase is coming from for later reference.

When to use a paraphrase

Deciding when to use a paraphrase instead of a quotation could be difficult, but a long paragraph full of quotations can be difficult to decipher, especially when the direct quotations are unnecessary. Sections that have ideas you would like to use are candidates for paraphrases if the author's original wording is not crucial. Sentences from a source might only have bits and pieces that apply directly to your topic or use more jargon and detail

than what is needed for your paper. These are also times to use a paraphrase.

Citations and paraphrasing

Paraphrases are trickier to cite than quotations, but not by much. Because paraphrases are not defined by the boundary of quotation marks, telling where a paraphrase starts or finishes can be more difficult. Citations for paraphrases should go at the end of the paraphrased sentence or sentences. When referencing specific numbers or statistics within the paraphrase, you might want to include a footnote directly following the number so the reader can check that specific statistic in the source, but this is not a requirement. The citation can also go at the end of the sentence. A long as you obviously are citing the information from the paraphrase, it is not as crucial where the citation goes. It should not matter how long your paraphrase is. If the entire paraphrase is coming from the same source, you will only need one citation, not a parenthetical reference or footnote at the end of every sentence in a paraphrase. An exception to this would be if you included a personal aside or explanation that is not taken from the source in the middle of a paraphrase. *Further details about citation methods and common citation styles and examples will be discussed in Chapter 7.*

Summarizing

Summaries are often confused with paraphrases, but they are subtly different. Summarizing is closer to paraphrasing than quoting but covers a wider spread of information than a paraphrase would. Paraphrases involve taking a few sentences or a paragraph you might otherwise have quoted and putting it into your own words. Summarizing, on the other hand, gives an overview of key points from several paragraphs or possibly even an entire chapter or article. The usefulness of summaries will depend on the topic of your research paper and the scope it is meant to cover. If the intended audience is someone with little or no knowledge of your topic, summaries are a way to condense relevant ideas and make them manageable.

When using summaries, beware of condensing too much information into a small space. Summaries allow you to quickly inform the reader of several key points from a much larger piece, but they can be hazardous for these same reasons. Summarizing a large amount of technical information could confuse readers or make them feel inundated. Always make summaries easy to follow. It can be tempting to show off your knowledge by using technical or academic language geared toward impressing professors, but keeping explanations simple is often much better. Using straightforward and simple explanations in a summary gets the point across and proves you know what you are talking about well enough to explain it to people who might not be as familiar with the topic. If you are not sure whether a summary is out of control, run it past a friend or roommate to see whether he or she can follow the information.

Tip No. **50** **Summaries condense and paraphrases clarify.**

It can be hard to decide whether you are better off using a paraphrase or a summary. Little difference exists in the mechanics of how to cite each one within your paper, but there is a difference in how you write them. A good rule to follow is paraphrases are a way to clarify a piece of information that you otherwise would have quoted, especially in reference to your thesis statement. A summary condenses information for the sake of giving an overview or saving space when an in-depth explanation is not necessary to make your point.

When to use a summary

Whenever you want to condense several pieces of information from multiple places within a source, a summary is your best bet. This is especially true for papers written for a reader unfamiliar with the topic though they can be useful in other situations. Use summaries to give background information or cover key facts the reader needs to understand to appreciate the technical aspects of your argument. While researching,

you often will have to read pages of information just to gain a proper understanding of a vital factor that relates to your topic. If readers need to understand something to fully appreciate an aspect of your paper, your job as the writer is to give them an abridged version. Summaries are often the best way of doing that.

Citations and summarizing

Summaries are the most difficult to cite properly because of their nature. They lack the obvious boundaries quotations have, and unlike paraphrases, they often draw on several paragraphs or pages of information. They might also use information from more than one source. For these reasons, figuring out where to  put citations and what to include in these citations can be confusing and frustrating. To simplify this, use the following guidelines on where to put your citations:

- If your summary draws from a single source and a single location within that source, such as one or two pages within a chapter, cite it the same way you would a paraphrase with a single notation or parenthetical reference.

- If your summary draws from several places throughout the same source, such as multiple chapters, put a citation for each of these locations next to the piece of information taken from that spot. The reader will be able to find this information within the source if he or she chooses to look for it. Do not use this method if you are using a citation format that does not require you to give page numbers. *For examples of which formats require page numbers, see Chapter 7.*

- If your summary takes information from multiple sources, such as statistics that relate to each other from multiple documents, you must include citations corresponding to each source after the part of the summary taken from that source. Otherwise, the reader will not be able to tell which piece of information came from which source.

This will take time to get the hang of, but as long as you look at your citations and continue to ask yourself whether the citation clearly corresponds to your information, you should have no problem placing your citations correctly. *Specific details on formatting citations and examples of citations are given in Chapter 7.*

Study Guide

- Plagiarism is taking the intellectual property of another author and presenting it as your own work.

  - You can still use information from your research in your paper; you just need to give credit to the original author with a citation.

  - Even if you do not think you are presenting someone else's work as your own, it can still be considered plagiarism if you do not cite the work properly.

- Plagiarism is a serious offense in the academic world with real consequences, such as failure and expulsion.

  - Due to copyright laws, you might even face legal action for plagiarism.

- You must give credit for every quote, paraphrase, summary, statistic, and other idea you get from another source.

  - When in doubt, use a citation. If you have to ask yourself whether something needs a citation, assume the answer is yes.

  - Information on types of citations will be discussed in detail in Chapter 7.

- The three most common ways to use research to support your argument are quotations, paraphrases, and summaries.

- Quotations insert another author's exact words into your paper.

  - Quotations are best used to highlight information that is worded well and supports your thesis without having to make any changes.

- Paraphrases take a specific statement you otherwise might have quoted and put it into your own words.

  - Paraphrases are a way to clarify information so the way it relates to your thesis is clear.

- Summaries are like paraphrases, but they cover and condense a broader spectrum of information.

  - Summaries can give an overview of information from several locations within the same source or even multiple sources as long as you give a citation for each part of the summary.

CHAPTER 7

Citation Methods

Citations intimidate many students for a few good reasons. Many teachers and professors drill the importance of proper citations and the risks of plagiarism. There are several different methods for citing sources, and graders are often strict and will dock points for misplaced periods or commas in citations. Also, keeping track of sources, authors, page numbers, publishers, and dates on top of all the other information you need for your paper can be stressful, time-consuming, and tedious.

Tip No. 51 Consider investing in a style guide booklet.

Some colleges require you to buy a style guide or writer's handbook, but if your school does not, the book is still a worthwhile investment. Ask around, and figure out which format you will be using most frequently during your studies. Go to the bookstore and find a style guide specifically for that format. Although the tips and tricks in the book you have in front of you will get you started, having a handy desk guide that goes into more depth than this book has the room to do will be useful. Alternately, many web sources have guides to the various styles, so if you are more tech savvy, bookmark a few web guides for later reference.

Citations can be a hassle, but once you learn how, citing sources becomes much less intimidating. Although there are several different methods for citing sources, they all share commonalities that make learning a new citation method easier. Also, depending on your

chosen field of study in college, you will likely only need to be intimately familiar with one format. Regardless of the format or the aspect of it that intimidates you, this chapter will give you a crash course in the three most common citation methods for college papers. For the sake of illustration, the same three fictional sources will be given as samples in each section to highlight the similarities and differences among the styles. One will be a book, one an article, and one a website because these are the most common types of citations you will be using. Different types of sources are cited differently, so if you need to cite a less common type of source, use a style guide or citation generator to make sure you get the format right. This chapter focuses on citations in your text. *For information on bibliography formats, see Chapter 11.*

Style Guides: What Are They, and How Are They Used?

A style guide is a handbook that contains the rules and conventions for a particular writing format. Style guides are extremely handy to have on hand because you never know when you are going to run across something new that you will have to figure out how to properly reference. They make troubleshooting while working on citations much easier because they go into more depth than a book about writing papers will.

You can get free access to guides for the major styles online. You might want to bookmark these sites in your Web browser for later reference. If you are the type who likes to have information hard copy, purchase a style manual for whichever style you will be using most frequently. Most major bookstores have entire sections dedicated to writing papers, and they will contain guides for every major writing style plus some more obscure ones. Peruse these, and keep in mind all of the style guides will have similar information. Look for one laid out in a way that is easy for you to navigate. Keep the style guide on your desk for easy reference while writing papers.

Alternately, if you want to have a hard copy but do not have the cash to shell out for a style manual, purchase a cheap binder from a department store and print out excerpts from the online style guides. Put them in the binder, and mark them up with your own notations and reminders. You can always print a new one later.

MLA Format

Modern Language Association (MLA) format might already be familiar to some students entering college. Some high schools use it as their default paper-writing format, and you might have had to use it in an English or composition course. MLA is most commonly used in English classes but is often the default style for all humanities and modern language classes. Because MLA is associated with the humanities, and humanities classes tend to assign more papers than others, it is worth taking time to familiarize yourself with the format regardless of your field of study.

A Note to Non-English Majors

Doing projects for classes outside your chosen major can be frustrating, and some students dread it. Many scientifically minded individuals have difficulty with English classes and paper-writing in general though lab reports might bother them less. But as a college student, you will be required to fill out your transcript with general education classes to meet graduation requirements. This will include English, history, and other humanities courses. You will be hard-pressed to get out of college without having to write an English paper at some point. For this reason, it might behoove you to at least briefly familiarize yourself with MLA format on top of whichever format your chosen major predominantly uses. It will give you one fewer worry when you write that dreaded English paper.

The MLA in-text citation

MLA format uses parenthetical in-text citations. Parenthetical means your citation will be enclosed with parentheses. Inside the parentheses, include the last name of the author and the page number, or numbers, the information being cited was taken from. The author's last name will come first followed by the page number. When citing poetry, use the line number rather than a page number. Do not place a comma between the author's last name and the page number. The citation should also go at the end of the information cited but before the terminal punctuation, a period in most cases. In the cases of particularly short papers or literary analysis not involving any secondary sources, you might only have one location you are drawing information from. In this case, you might use just a page number within the parentheses.

Sample MLA citations

Here are three sample citations from three different sources. A quote taken from page 15 of John Doe's book *Why Getting Citations Right is Really Important* would be presented as follows:

```
"There is no excuse for getting a citation
wrong," (Doe 15).
```

If this quote came from a scholarly journal rather than a book, the in-text citation would look exactly the same:

```
"There is no excuse for getting a citation
wrong," (Doe 15).
```

The only difference if the quote came from a website is the website has no pagination, so there is no page number to reference:

```
"There is no excuse for getting a citation
wrong," (Doe).
```

As with the website, you will occasionally run into sources that do not have all of the information you would generally use for a citation. It would be impossible to cover every single exception in this book, so when you run into trouble, check an MLA style guide. One is available for free online as part of the Purdue Online Writing Lab (OWL) and can be found at **http://owl.english.purdue.edu/owl/resource/747/01**.

> **Tip No. 52** **Familiarize yourself with more than one citation method if possible.**
>
> You might only need to know one format inside and out for your major, but you will inevitably have to take classes outside your major. Professors will allow you to use whichever citation method you want, but many will prefer or require you to write papers in the standard format for that discipline. For this reason, spend time looking over the basics for all three of the citation methods covered in this chapter. It will make the prospect of having to write a physics report as an English major, or vice versa, less daunting when and if the time comes.

APA Format

APA Format is similar to MLA in its origins, but the American Psychological Association authored this style. For this reason, psychology and the social sciences most commonly used this format though you might run into it in the other sciences. APA and Chicago or Turabian style are used in many of the same disciplines, so it can be a tossup as to which you will use more. Ask around at your school to find out which one is preferred if you are not sure.

The APA in-text citation

Much like MLA, APA style makes use of parenthetical in-text citations. The biggest difference between a MLA parenthetical reference and an APA parenthetical reference is APA gives the author's last name and the year the piece was published rather than a page number. Unlike MLA, APA also includes a comma between the author's last name and the year.

> **Tip No.**
> # 53 Pay attention to your commas and periods.
> When it comes to citations, the little details make a big difference. It might be hard to believe, but placing a period in the wrong spot or putting a comma in a citation where it does not belong can cost you points. Enough small errors can add up to a lower letter grade, so mind your punctuation.

Sample APA citations

Here are the same three sample citations used in the MLA section, but this time they will be presented in APA format. The same quote taken from page 15 of John Doe's book *Why Getting Citations Right is Really Important*, published in 2011, would be presented as follows:

```
"There is no excuse for getting a citation
wrong," (Doe, 2011).
```

As an article from a scholarly journal with the same publication year, the in-text citation would look exactly the same:

> "There is no excuse for getting a citation wrong," (Doe, 2011).

If the quote came from a website, the publication year would be the year the website was last updated. If this information is not available, substitute a page number or paragraph number. Include the abbreviation "n.d." to signify no date. In this case, assume the quote is from the third paragraph in the text.

> "There is no excuse for getting a citation wrong," (Doe, n.d., para 3).

If you are giving a specific piece of information, you might include a page number in the parenthetical as well. Use your discretion. It would be impossible for this text to cover what to do in every situation, so if you are missing information that would normally be included in the citation, use a style guide to troubleshoot the problem. The APA also has an extensive APA Format Frequently Asked Questions section on their website, which can be found at **www.apastyle.org**.

Tip No. 54

In-text citations will vary a lot less than bibliographic entries.

Many of these citations look similar, and it might seem there is little difference between citing different types of sources. In the body of the paper, this is true. In some cases, missing information could make these citations different, but for the most part, they are simple. The real differences will become clear when you put together your reference list, bibliography, or works cited page. *See Chapter 11 for details.*

Turabian or Chicago Style

The last style this book will cover is Turabian Style, sometimes referred to as Chicago Manual or Chicago Style. Although the two styles have some subtle differences, they are almost identical, and some people use the terms interchangeably. Kate Turabian originally developed the Turabian Style for the University of Chicago. This style is based on the Chicago Manual of Style (CMS) but focuses more specifically on writing college papers, theses, and dissertations.

The Chicago/Turabian in-text citation

This style is more confusing than MLA or APA because it can use either parenthetical citations or footnotes depending on the situation. There is no hard and fast rule for which papers use parenthetical references and which use footnotes, so be sure to ask the professor which he or she prefers if it is not made clear.

The parenthetical citations are a sort of cross between MLA and APA citations. They will include a publication date and a page number and the author's last name. The author's last name will come first followed by the year and then the page number. There should be no comma between the author's last name and the date, but do include a comma between the date and the page number.

If you are using the footnote citation method, insert a footnote where you would like to put your citation. A feature in your word processing program allows you to do this. In Microsoft Word and many other word processors, the footnote tool can be found under the insert menu. The footnote will include a superscript number after the piece of information being cited.

This will then lead the reader to a bibliographic reference for the source of the information. *More detail on how to format this part of a footnote will be covered in Chapter 11.*

Sample Chicago/Turabian in-text citations

Here are the same three sample citations used in the MLA and APA sections, but this time they will be presented in Chicago format. Our quote from page 15 of John Doe's 2011 book *Why Getting Citations Right is Really Important* would be presented as follows:

```
"There is no excuse for getting a citation
wrong," (Doe 2011, 15).
```

As a journal article with the same publication year and pagination, it would be identical.

```
"There is no excuse for getting a citation
wrong," (Doe 2011, 15).
```

Websites often do not have publication dates. If this is the case, substitute the date the website was accessed. If there is no pagination, and there likely will not be, do not include it.

```
"There is no excuse for getting a citation
wrong," (Doe 2011).
```

No matter where the information is coming from, your in-text footnote will look the same. You will have a quote or paraphrase followed by a superscript number:

"There is no excuse for getting a citation wrong."[1]

The entry the footnote leads to will vary based on the type of source. *For details on this, refer to Chapter 11.* For a more in-depth look at this citation method, check out **www.chicagomanualofstyle.org** or **www.press.uchicago.edu/books/turabian/turabian_citationguide.html**.

Citation Machines

Technology moves at a lightning pace, and with spell checkers, plagiarism-detecting software, and computerized note-taking software becoming standard, it should come as no surprise there are automated citation tools. Although you should never completely rely on a tool like this because it is not foolproof, citation machines can be helpful when you are on a tight deadline or have to put together citations in a style you have never used before. Citation machines ask you to input the information needed for a citation in a particular style and then generate a formatted citation for you that you can copy directly into your paper. Son of Citation Machine at **http://citationmachine.net** is a website for this. It is free to use and can generate citations in MLA, APA, Turabian, and Chicago styles.

CASE STUDY: LEARNING STYLES AND ASKING FOR ASSISTANCE

Rochelle DeJarlais
Student
University of Wisconsin—Whitewater

I have completed three years of college. I wrote papers during those three years and through my high school career. It seems I learn more about writing with each class I take. Even though I am an accounting major, I still need to know how to write, not just crunch numbers.

Based on the experience that I have had with papers, a great paper is one that has correct grammar and spelling. Getting grammar and spelling correct is so easy to do. The computer does that for you, but there always seems to be some errors that make it into papers. The computer spell-checker does not catch all grammar mistakes, so the writer needs to go back through and look for grammar errors.

If you are a new college student and have never written a college paper before, go to your professor and ask for help. Ask what he or she is looking for in the paper. There might be some key points he or she wants to see you write about so you can fully show your understanding. Also, your campus might have a writing lab or someone in the college library who can help with writing papers.

It is also important to know which form the professor wants the paper in. The two most popular writing forms are MLA and APA. If you are writing a research paper that needs a works cited page or bibliography at the end with all the sources you used to write the paper, it is important to know which writing style is needed. The works cited or bibliography will look different and need different information depending on the writing form.

If you have been struggling with writing research papers for a long time, now is the time to get help. I can't remember how many papers and research papers I have written during my college career, but there has been a handful. If you are having trouble, go to the writing lab on campus or go to the professor for help. If you need help with grammar, you can go on the Purdue Owl website. They have exercises to help with grammar. They also have information about the MLA and APA style.

Before writing a paper, make sure you know what you want the reader or audience to get out of it. Why should they read this? Make sure the topic is appropriate for the target audience. For example, an age group of older than 60 would not be interested in reading about applying for financial aid.

If you are a procrastinator and don't like writing papers, you need to get out of that cycle. The day you find out about a paper assignment, you should already be thinking about which topic you are going to write about. Do a part of the paper each day until the due date. You will not get a good grade if you start it the night before. College papers are not like high school papers. You might accompany college papers with a presentation with visuals, and you sometimes will include in your paper visuals, such as graphs, tables, or appendices. A lot of work goes into these types of assignments, and you need to give yourself as much time as possible.

Study Guide

- The three most common citation formats are MLA, APA, and Turabian or Chicago style.

- Having a passing familiarity with all of these styles will save you time if you have to write a paper outside your discipline and in a different style.

- MLA format is used most frequently in papers for English, humanities, and modern language.

  - Uses parenthetical citations that include the author's last name and the page number with no comma.

- APA format is used most frequently in psychology and social sciences.

  - Uses parenthetical citations that include the author's last name and the year of publication separated by a comma.

- Turabian or Chicago style is used most frequently in natural sciences but can show up in social sciences as well.

  - Uses either parenthetical references or footnotes.

  - Parenthetical citations should include the author's last name, the year of publication, and the page number with a comma between the year and page number.

  - Footnotes will have a superscript number after the information being cited that corresponds to a bibliographic information entry.

CHAPTER 8

Writing the Introduction

Once all the prep work is over, it is time to sit down and write the paper. It might seem as though you have spent an exorbitant amount of time planning for the paper, but all the work you completed up to this

point will start paying off. You would have done the prep work anyway while staring at a blank word processor screen and feeling frustrated without any organization or guidance. Now the guesswork has been taken out, writing an introduction and then the rest of the paper will be much more straightforward.

For many people, getting started is the most difficult part. Writing introductions can be intimidating. Many students do not know what they should include in an introduction that will properly lead into the paper and still have enough pizzazz to be interesting. Some students will even skip writing the introduction when starting their papers and come back to it later. Nothing is wrong with skipping around while writing, but waiting to write the introduction until the end can leave you with a poorly written setup to an otherwise well-written paper. Although this might not completely ruin a paper, it does not do it any favors. The introduction is the first impression readers get of your paper, and if they do not like it, they will not want to keep reading. Your professor will have to read the entire paper regardless, but your professor is also far more likely to remember and give high marks to a paper that was impressive from the first lines.

Tip No. **55** Give yourself a filler introduction before jumping into the body of your paper.

If you are having trouble putting together an introduction that sings, force yourself to at least write a placeholder that sets up your paper. It is acceptable if this placeholder is not as strong as you would like it to be because you can come back later and edit it, but having a brief introduction that sets up the direction of the paper will help you as you write. Do not forget to go back and fix it before you turn the paper in.

What to Include

Deciding what to include in an introduction is the most intimidating part of writing one. A proper introduction draws readers in while providing the setup for the entire paper. Think of putting together your introduction as setting up a row of dominoes. If done correctly, your introduction should set everything up in the reader's mind and in yours so when it comes time to write the body of the paper, you just have to knock the first domino over and watch everything fall into place. A good introduction should do each of the following:

- Hook the reader and pique interest in the topic.
- Provide background information to further draw the reader in.
- Give the reader a general knowledge of what the paper is about.
- Preview key points and lead into the thesis statement.

Some writing instructors or guides might present you with a formula for writing an introduction, and although these can be useful, your papers can get stale if they all start the same way. Moreover, these might not be appropriate for every subject. Rather than give a formula, this chapter will go over what makes an introduction good. There is no single way to write an introduction that will always work for every topic, but these points should act as a guide.

Writing the hook

The first sentence of the paper is crucial. If you are at all skeptical, think back to all the research you have done. Were there any articles you skipped over after reading only one sentence or two because they did not grab you enough to make you want to use them for your research? If so, you should already realize that by failing to make a paper appealing right from the start, the reader will become disinterested. The same can be said of novels and movies. So, how do you draw a reader in and engage them in your topic?

Tip No.

56 Consider your ideal reader.
An ideal reader is the hypothetical perfect reader for your paper. Your professor will be the one ultimately reading your paper, but that does not automatically mean your professor is your ideal reader. You might have been instructed to write the paper as though someone with no prior knowledge on the subject were going to read it, or you might be asked to assume your reader is already familiar. Consider these points, and once you know the knowledge level and interests your ideal reader would have, tailor your introduction and the rest of the paper to meet the needs of this imaginary reader.

Starting with a question or a quotation is a common answer, but these types of hooks have become overused and clichéd. Take caution leading into your paper using one of those methods. The best way to find a hook is to compose a sentence that is broad and interesting and segues nicely into your argument. A paper that opens with a broad or sweeping statement instead of one specifically related to your main point will appeal to a wider audience. This will allow you reel the reader in as you direct his or her attention to the main point of your paper. If you are having difficulty coming up with something to grab the reader's attention, consider making a list of what is interesting about your topic. Are there any current events it relates to or controversies associated with it that might be points of interest? Consider who the paper is aimed at informing, and then come up with why that hypothetical reader would be interested in your paper. Devise an opening sentence that would appeal to them.

Using the Inverted Pyramid

Keep in mind the inverted pyramid, or upside-down triangle while laying out your introduction. Just as an inverted pyramid is widest at the top and narrows to a point, your introduction should start out broad and then narrow down to your specific topic and thesis statement. You can vary this formula, especially after you get the hang of writing research papers, but always be sure to narrow down to your thesis statement. Even if you do not start out broad, make sure your introduction complements your thesis statement and leads into it without seeming choppy or forced. It is the main point of your paper, and you have likely spent a lot of time perfecting it. Make sure you have an introduction that allows it to shine.

Providing background information

Starting out with broad statements to draw readers in can also serve the purpose of informing readers about background topics that relate to the specific issue you are writing about. A proper introduction needs to contain enough background material to allow the reader to understand the thesis statement and the paper's arguments. There is no need to go into too much detail at this stage, but giving a brief overview of information pertaining to your research is helpful for the reader. For this reason, introductions are a good place to include summaries. *For more information on summaries, refer to Chapter 6.*

The amount of background information required will depend on the topic. A research paper about a specific historical incident might require more setup than a literary analysis though there are literary pieces that require an explanation of the author's motivations or the context in which it was written. There is a fine line you must walk when using background information. Do not give so much it becomes boring or uninteresting, but include enough so you do not have to spend too much time giving background information in the body of your paper. Summarizing in the introduction is far more effective. Use your best judgment for how much background information to include. If you are unsure, here are a few questions to help you decide:

1. **Is there any historical context that is important in understanding this topic?**

   Look at the events that shaped the history of your topic. Did significant scientific studies eventually lead to the topic you have chosen? Did an important court case create the issue your paper tackles? Did the time period in which an author was born heavily shape one of his or her stories? These are all details that you might consider including in an introduction.

2. **Are there any larger or better-known issues that relate to or lead directly to this topic?**

   When you did your prewriting, you had to narrow your topic into something that was easier to grapple with in the space allowed for the assignment. Think back to that larger topic, and ask yourself whether any better-known issues are connected to or directly led to the topic you are covering. This is especially useful to consider when writing a paper about a topic that is not widely known. Connecting it to something your readers might know more about will draw them in and help them understand why this topic is important.

3. Is there any biographical information that gives a better understanding of this topic?

Depending on the topic, key people might be involved in it. Authors, scientists, historical figures, or politicians are examples. If any figure or group plays a key role in your topic, consider whether biographical information about the person or group would be useful for the reader. These details often might not be important in the body of the paper, but they make good tidbits to include in an introduction.

4. Are there any statistics or other significant details that would give the reader a better understanding of why this topic is important?

Other statistics or ideas might help illustrate why your topic is important and worth reading about. Some of these might have even given you the idea for the paper to begin with. Ultimately, anything that gets the reader's attention and highlights the importance of your topic can become an introduction, so go over your notes again for information that might work.

5. Does any information fit better later in the paper?

You do not want to use all of the crucial bits of information in your introduction. If your research paper focuses heavily on the biography of a politician or author, it might be unwise to use too much biographical information in your introduction. It will steal your thunder later on. Look for information that seems important and leads into your topic but does not necessarily fit in with a later section of the paper. You do not want to weaken your arguments later. You want to introduce them using information that will whet the reader's appetite.

6. **Can this information be presented in a way that draws readers into this topic?**

If the information you are coming up with seems boring or unlikely to grab the reader's attention, play with it to see whether you can word it in a way that makes it catchier or more interesting. The whole point of an introduction is to launch into your topic in a way that makes the reader want to keep reading. If you cannot find a way to do this with the background information you are considering, you are much better off looking for different information to use. Proper presentation can make almost anything interesting, but it can take significant practice to become adept at that presentation. Experiment with it because you can always scrap an idea and try again.

The amount of background information you include is up to you. Practice is the only way to get a feel for how much to include in any given situation because it will vary from topic to topic. Make any piece of background information as succinct as possible, and do not be afraid to enlist the help of a writing tutor. They can discuss ideas with you and will be able to suggest when to include more or less background or make other improvements.

57 If you are having trouble making up your mind, write more than one.

This is not always feasible when you are running on a tight deadline, but if time allows and you are having difficulty deciding how to write your introduction, write more than one. If you have two or more ideas, jot them out quickly and then tuck them away for a few hours before looking them over again. One might stand out more than the other, or you might find you like ideas from both and can mix and match. If you still cannot make up your mind, ask for a second opinion or look at them again once you have written more of the paper.

Previewing key points for the rest of paper.

The introduction is a lot like the movie trailer for your paper. It should preview what is to come and interest the audience with enough of an understanding of the key points but still leave the best for the main event. It is always disappointing when you see a movie and all the best parts were already in the trailer. You might also see trailers for movies that look entertaining but have no idea of what the movie is about. You want to avoid giving the reader that feeling with your introduction. Your thesis will explain your main argument, but you might want to lead into the thesis by *briefly* bringing up a few of your main supporting details. Give the reader a taste of what is to come, but do not use the most compelling parts of your argument yet. Save those for the body of the paper. Always keep these previews as concise as possible. This will help you avoid giving away too much in the introduction.

Tip No.

58 An introduction should be all the reader needs to summarize your paper.

A good introduction will allow a reader to tell someone what your paper is about before he or she even reads the rest of the paper. It should not give away all the details but should set up the argument and allow readers to accurately describe it to someone. You can test this by having a friend read your introduction and then tell you what they think your paper will discuss. If your friend's guess is close to what you had planned on covering, you are doing well. If not, consider some revisions, and ask your friend which parts misled or confused him or her.

Leading into the thesis statement

Remember that thesis statement you spent so much time on? This is what all that work was for. Your introduction is just a lead into your thesis, which then leads into the rest of your paper. Look at your thesis and the points you bring up in it. Make sure you lead into these points and explain any jargon or concepts that are not common knowledge. An otherwise successful thesis statement can still fall flat if it is not introduced properly. Make sure the sentences leading up to the thesis statement are clearly worded and strong. In addition, double-check that nothing before your thesis statement changes the context of the statement. Consider taking a key word or two from your thesis and including it in the sentence directly before it. Avoid being redundant, but you can ensure a proper transition from the start of the introduction to the thesis with this technique.

Important Note Before Proceeding

Your paper's thesis statement should already be written at this stage. If the thesis statement is not written, however, it is imperative to write one before continuing with your paper. Without a thesis statement, your paper will lack cohesion and a solid direction. If you have written your thesis already, give it another once-over and make any necessary changes. If you have not edited your thesis at all during the course of your research, it might need a few tweaks based on the additional information on the subject you are now equipped with. For the same reasons you do not want to proceed writing your paper without a thesis statement, be sure your thesis has undergone any necessary edits before diving into writing the body of the paper. This is not to say you cannot come back to it later and make further changes, but it will be far easier to flow everything smoothly and logically if your thesis is solid now. *For more details on how to write a thesis statement, see Chapter 3*

Effective Introduction Techniques

Tip No.

59 Use the search engine test to find clichés.

If you are having trouble deciding whether something is a cliché, an easy way to tell is to type the phrase into your search engine of choice. If there are tons of results with the exact same or similar wording, you probably have a cliché on your hands. If you get few results or results that do not phrase the information the same way as you do in the paper, the chances of it being a cliché decrease.

Now that you know which elements make up a successful introduction, here are a few techniques to use if you get stuck figuring out where to start and a few to avoid. Here is your list of do's and don'ts for putting together an introduction:

Do:

- Consider starting with an amusing anecdote or story relating to your topic. These are interesting to readers and can give background information on the topic.

- Look for shocking or unusual facts or statistics related to your topic to use in your introduction. Surprising readers is a way to get them interested and can set up for extrapolation that will lead them into your thesis.

- Think about using humor when appropriate. Some topics are more somber and would not lend themselves to this technique, but if your topic is more lighthearted, tasteful and witty statements can hooks readers.

- Consider starting with a vividly detailed description of a person, place, or event that is central to your topic. For students with a creative or artistic side, a dramatization to set the scene for a paper can work well and be fun to write.

Don't:

- Start with a famous quotation or any quotation. It can be tempting to begin with a quotation you found in your research, but you are better off crafting an introduction with your own words.

- Begin with a question. This can be done sparingly, but starting the introduction off with a question has become cliché. If you want to use a question to lead into your introduction, start with a statement that leads into the question and then ask the question a few sentences into the introduction.

- Use recipe metaphors. These statements treat elements of the topic like ingredients in a recipe. They read something like, "Take a large quantity of X, add Y, and sprinkle with Z, and you get this topic." This format has become gimmicky and cliché.

- Include any other clichés or gimmicks in your introduction. If you are unsure whether something is cliché, ask around to see whether other people have heard something similar before. Alternately, type phrases into your search engine of choice and see what comes back. If you return a large number of hits, the idea likely  is overdone, and you will need to either come up with something more original or find a way to put a new twist on the cliché.

Reinventing the Cliché

You use clichés every single day whether you realize it. Clichés are overused turns of phrase that have become tired, trite, or boring. These are so ingrained in our language they will turn up in your writing at some point. Because they are so common, looking for them in your writing can feel like looking for a needle in a haystack. When used sparingly, they do not ruin your paper, but look for any clichés that might have snuck in when you go back and reread your writing. Variety is the spice of life, and clichés are anything but. Clichés are expected, and they will often flow naturally into sentences. If you spot a cliché, be aware of it and consider changing it. Most clichés were, at one point, new and funny. They were so well-liked they became overused and have lost much of their humor and intelligence. Going through your writing and highlighting all the clichés that you find is like beating a dead horse. You will grow as a writer if you replace these clichés with new and more inventive phrasing. The removal of the cliché will make the writing better and will likely get your point across more clearly. You can even play with the cliché to show you are aware of it but have chosen to alter it slightly to make it new and fresh. Play around with the words, and see what you come up with and how much better it makes your writing.

For example, the phrases "needle in a haystack," "variety is the spice of life," and "beating a dead horse" are all clichés and should be reworded. "Variety is the spice of life" might be reworked to say, "diversifying your sentences is more creative as well as more fun." Be creative, get out a thesaurus if needed, and use your own words.

Sample Introduction

The following is a sample introduction from a paper written about the theme of madness in literature as portrayed in Edgar Allan Poe's short story *The Tell-Tale Heart*.

Much of art involved exploring the depths and mysteries of the human mind, from motivations to emotions and even insanity. In fact, many writers seemed to have an intuitive understanding of mental illnesses such as depression, bipolar, and schizophrenia long before they were recognized and defined as conditions. The motif of the descent into madness is one that recurs in art and literature throughout the ages. It can be found in the guilt-torn mind of Shakespeare's Lady Macbeth and the horrors explored in the works of H.P. Lovecraft. Few authors are as famous for writing Gothic tales of madness and horror, however, as Edgar Allan Poe. Many consider Poe to be one of the fathers of the modern Gothic tale, and his reinterpretation of internal horror has influenced countless writers since. Although Poe uses these themes in several of his works, *The Tell-Tale Heart* is a particularly poignant exploration of the personal horror of madness that is even more poignant when viewed in conjunction with modern psychological advances. The narrator repeatedly assures the reader he is not mad, but he is trying to convince himself of this as each instance further illuminates his insanity.

Study Guide

- Introductions can seem tricky, but once you know what makes a successful introduction, they become simple.

- A good introduction will do all of the following:

  - Hook the reader and pique interest in the topic.

  - Provide background information to further draw in the reader.

  - Give the reader a general idea of what the paper is about.

  - Preview key points and lead into the thesis statement.

- Consider using an anecdote, surprising fact, a dash of humor, or a detailed description to hook the reader.

- Look for background information that might not fit in with the rest of your paper but still be good for the reader to know, and consider using it in your introduction.

  - Be sure to include any background information that the reader needs for understanding your thesis statement.

- Think of the introduction as a movie trailer. You want to let the reader know what the paper is about and preview your key points without giving away all the best parts.

- Make sure everything in the introduction ultimately leads into the thesis statement and provides the proper context for it.

- Use the inverted pyramid. Start general or broad, and then narrow to your specific thesis statement.

- Avoid gimmicks and clichés in the introduction. Your professor is reading several papers at once, so he or she is well-versed in recognizing overused techniques.

CHAPTER 9

Writing the Body of Your Paper

With your introduction completed, you can move on to the heart of your paper. If your prep work didn't all pay off while writing your introduction, the body is where it will start to make a difference. The body of your paper is everything between the introduction and the conclusion. You have freedom when it comes to writing the body of your paper, which can be liberating and frightening. More freedom means more room to experiment and do what you like, but it also means less guidance and more room to make mistakes. There are as many  ways to write the body of a paper as there are papers, but even so, here are some basic guidelines to make writing the bulk of your paper easier:

Tip No. 60   **Keep all the work you have done so far handy to keep yourself from getting lost traversing the middle of your paper.**

The middle of the paper can be dangerous grounds for the underprepared. Losing your point or writing in circles while you figure out what you want to say is easy. Do not let this happen to you. You are armed with a thesis statement, notecards, and solid outline, so you will have little chance of getting lost. If you see your sentences start to drift off topic, go back to these guides, figure out where you started to diverge from the path, and fix it.

While writing the body of your paper, keep all of the following in mind:

- Make sure your body supports the claims made in your thesis statement.
- Use cited research to support each of your points.
- Explain how the research you are citing supports your argument.
- Develop a rhythm for writing the paper.
- Use your thesis statement and outline in combination to guide your writing.
- Be sure to include transitions between each paragraph in the body.

The rest is ultimately up to you to write, but these tools will help keep you on track and elevate your writing to the next level. The rest of this chapter will examine each of these points in more detail.

Support Thesis Claims

Your body needs to support your thesis statement. Every point you make should go back to your thesis. At each turn, ask yourself how it relates to your thesis. If your body does not adequately support the thesis, the paper has failed. The thesis is your main argument, and you must provide enough evidence to back it up. This point seems obvious, but it is absolutely vital, and you would be surprised by how many students deviate from their theses in the bodies and do not sufficiently supporting their original arguments. How do you make sure you adequately support your thesis?

Use details for support

Your thesis statement should be argumentative in nature. *For more details on how to accomplish this, see Chapter 3.* Until now, everything you have done has been general. You have been generating ideas, pulling information from sources, forming opinions, and drafting an outline of what you plan to say. What all of that has lacked are details supporting these opinions and ideas. Flesh out these points using specific examples. Expound upon the claims you are making in your thesis. Why do you believe what your thesis is arguing? Which information has led you to form the opinions you have? Look at the points you are planning on covering, and write out the specific details that support these points in relation to your thesis. Take out your notecards, and if you have not already grouped them by topic, do so. Each opinion you plan on presenting in your paper should have one, if not several, specific details that you are planning on using to support it. Specific details can include examples, statistics, and data from experiments. Key in on details that show readers why your point is valid rather than tell them they should believe what you are saying.

Show Versus Tell:

If you have taken writing classes or involved yourself in writing workshops, you have probably heard someone refer to showing rather than telling. Some of your professors might even bring this up during lectures. This is commonly addressed in creative writing pursuits but is equally applicable to writing academically. Showing is always better than telling, but what exactly does that mean, and why is one better than the other?

Tell	Show
Telling is when you directly tell the reader a fact or opinion and they have to assume that this is true based on that statement.	Showing is when you present the reader with descriptions, details, and facts and let them draw conclusions based on that information.
"Chlorophyll absorbs sunlight and makes grass green."	"Grass, like most plants, takes in sunlight to produce essential nutrients. Chlorophyll absorbs sunlight, which triggers a chemical reaction within the plant to create the nutrients the plant needs to survive. Chlorophyll has a greenish hue, which is why healthy plants are generally green and dying or dead plants are not."

Showing can be risky because if you do not present the information properly, your readers might draw different conclusions than you would like them to. You can frame these details and descriptions in a way that guides the reader toward drawing the same conclusions you have and even say directly what your conclusions are, but readers will be better informed and more likely to accept what you are saying if they can see the information that has led you to this conclusion. Showing will also invariably require you to support your points with details, so it is also a useful exercise for that reason.

Use cited research

Properly using all the research you have done goes hand-in-hand with supporting your thesis. Most, if not all, of the details you use to support your claims will be taken directly from your notes in the form of statistics, quotes, paraphrases, and summaries. *For more information on the difference between quoting, paraphrasing, and summarizing, see Chapter 6.* Back up each point you make with your sources. This lends credibility to your argument and will prevent you from plagiarizing. *More information on plagiarism and its consequences can also be found in Chapter 6.*

Substantiate information with credible research

If you made a quotation outline or organized your notecards by topic, you likely have a good idea of the support you will be using to back up each of your main points and the source this information is coming from. *More information on organizing notecards and quotation outlines can be found in Chapter 5.* Understanding how this research ultimately fits into your paper is key at this stage. Each paragraph of your body should have its own topic or point. In your own words, introduce this idea and explain how it relates to your thesis. Once you have made a connection between this topic and your paper's main point, use examples from your research to substantiate the claims you have made. Drop in details from your notes, and finish by explaining how this detail furthers your argument. This last part will help ensure the reader understands which conclusions to draw from the information and does not confuse your point.

> **Tip No. 61 Be kind to your readers, but also be firm.**
> Assume your readers are intelligent, and do not condescend or talk down to them. Professors generally do not respond well to students who accidentally take this tone in their papers. Do not confuse treating the reader with respect and being gentle in your argument. Be firm when supporting your thesis without presuming to tell readers what to think. Instead, state facts and show how these facts agree with your argument.

You should have already checked your sources to make sure they are credible, but it is possible that as you start to write your paper, you discover a hole in your research. You might have a point that you want to include in your paper but cannot find anything to back it up in your other sources. You can go looking for new sources to corroborate your point; just be sure to check these sources the same way you checked the rest of them. Making a different point that might have less thunder but is backed up with credible sources is better than adding a piece of information at the last minute that turns out to be from a source that is not credible. If your credibility comes into question, even just on one point, readers will have a difficult time believing anything else about your argument. Damaging your credibility can doom an otherwise successful research paper. Now is also the time to double-check the context of your information to be sure you are not misrepresenting any information to further your points. *For more information on checking sources for credibility, see Chapter 4.*

Structuring a Paragraph

It might be helpful to think of each paragraph of your paper as a miniature paper. A good paragraph starts with a topic sentence, which acts as the thesis statement for an individual paragraph. A good topic sentence should focus the paragraph and give the reader an idea of what the paragraph will cover. This will also keep your writing focused on supporting the paragraph's main point and keep you from wandering away from your point. An individual paragraph should contain one well-supported main point. Aim for at least three supporting details in each paragraph. You might have more to include, but if you have fewer, your argument might not seem well-supported. Of course, this might change depending on the length and scope of the paper, but it is a good general rule.

An outline of a paragraph might look something like this:

1. Topic sentence
2. First supporting detail
3. Second supporting detail
4. Third supporting detail
5. Concluding/wrap-up sentence with a transition

If it helps, consider making outlines for each of your paragraphs, or use this as a tool to help organize paragraphs that are giving you trouble. This outline is an example and is not set in stone. Once you are comfortable writing paragraphs, you might occasionally deviate from these standard guidelines or use more or less support for the argument, but this provides a good starting point.

Include proper citations

Make sure you cite your research properly. Do not wait to put in citations until you are done with the paper even if it means interrupting your train of thought. If you made notecards or a spreadsheet with all your notes and citation information, this should not be difficult. If you did not, it is worth taking the time to stop and look up a page number or author as needed. If you wait to do citations until the end, you run the risk of forgetting to come back and finish the citation later. Even if you do not forget about your citations at the end, you could have trouble finding all the information you were planning on citing when you go back to it. This is especially true for papers that are several pages long and need many citations. Quotations are easy to spot, but paraphrases and summaries are not set apart from the rest of the text with quotation marks, so they are more difficult to find at a glance. You might also forget what was a paraphrase or summary when you come back to your paper after a hiatus. This is unacceptable, so take the time to put the citations in as you go. Once you get used to doing citations, they become second nature, so it does not take up any extra time and is worth the effort.

Tip No. 62 If you cannot put in a full citation at that time, put in a partial citation or use a place marker.

You might not be able to properly cite a piece of information while you are writing. Perhaps you forgot a book or set of notecards at home or you do not have the time to scour for a page number you forgot to write down. It happens to everyone. When you need to use a reference and cannot create a proper citation that moment, at least put in a partial citation. For MLA format, you can put in the parentheses and the author's name. If you need to make a footnote, you can start the footnote and make a note to come back to that spot later. Another useful trick is to use your word processor's highlight feature to highlight information that does not have a citation. This will make it easy to find when you come back to it later.

Develop a Rhythm

Writing a research paper has a rhythm to it. The more research papers you write, the better you will get at it. This is because the practice helps you establish a rhythm for writing a paper. Even if you are forced to write a paper on a topic you know little about or in a style that is unfamiliar to you, the rhythm of putting it together should not change much. Having a rhythm will help ensure your information flows neatly from point to point and paragraph to paragraph. You can vary the rhythm, but most paragraphs will follow these steps:

1. Start with a transition and topic sentence that introduce the main point of the paragraph.
2. Add more information to further explain the topic and how it relates to your thesis statement.
3. Back up what you have said so far with information from your sources.
4. Explain how the information you have cited supports your point(s) and adds credibility to your argument.
5. Add additional citations and explanations if you have more for the topic.
6. Repeat until you have covered all the points you are addressing in the paper.

Tip No. **63** Do not confuse a rhythm with monotony.
Getting into a groove while writing is no excuse to be boring. The best writers know the formats that are most compelling for arguing their points, but they present the information in such a way that it is not obvious they are following a formula. Getting a rhythm going will allow you to write faster, but it does not mean you have to format all of your sentences the same way. Do not fall into the trap of creating a laundry list of your points.

There is still plenty of room for variation on this theme, and the way you present this information is up to you. You have freedom with your presentation, so choose wording that fits with the type of paper you are writing and the subject matter. You might add lighthearted humor or keep things somber or extremely formal depending on the class and the topic. Find your voice, and write in a way that is comfortable for you. The basic skeleton underneath the writing will likely stay the same from paper to paper. For some, this might seem boring, but developing this rhythm will speed up your production and also give you a structure to go back to when you get stuck. People who talk about getting into a groove while writing, or having the words come easily so they can accomplish much in a short amount of time, have found a rhythm that allows this.

Tip No. 64 Your voice is where you are allowed to be creative, but make sure your tone matches the topic you are covering.

Many writers will talk about developing a style or voice. If you have a favorite author, you might be able to recognize his or her work by reading it without seeing the byline. This is because that author has developed a unique style that is easy to recognize. The more you write, the more you will find your own voice. Your personality partially dictates your voice. It might be easygoing, formal, witty, or comedic. Although using a voice will make your paper uniquely yours and allow you to be creative, be sure developing your voice and inserting some personality into your writing does not clash with the topic you are covering. Somber topics might not be suited to a humorous tone, and some classes might require a formal tone. You can still be creative; just make sure the creativity does not interfere with properly covering the topic at hand.

Follow Outline and Thesis Statement

Your outline and thesis statement are your guides for writing your paper, so refer back to them often. This will keep you on track and ensure you do not deviate from your points. Without an outline, writers often find themselves meandering away from their main points while they figure out what it is they want to say. Having an outline means you should never have to ask yourself what comes next. You should be able to look at your outline and have your answer. No matter which kind of outline you made, your main points should be listed in some fashion. Whenever you slow down or find yourself at a loss for what comes next, find the next point on your outline and start writing about it.

Tip No. **65** Look to your outline to craft your topic sentences.

Depending on the type of outline you made and the amount of work you put into it, you likely have the basis for some, if not all, the topic sentences you need for your paper already started. A topic sentence is a miniature thesis statement and should tell the reader the paragraph they are about to read will cover. When you start a new paragraph, your outline should be the first place you look. Once you have the paragraph's topic sentence written, the rest of the paragraph should flow easily.

Also often refer back to your thesis statement. Each paragraph should address something related to your thesis. Having it handy ideally will help you avoid getting stuck while addressing that part of each paragraph. Your outline likely will contain the start to many, if not all, the topic sentences for each paragraph of your paper. You can then add details, clarify these ideas, and pull up the research you will be using to support these points. If you are unsure of the research you should have ready for the next part of your paper, refer to your outline. Referring back to an outline also makes it much easier to develop the rhythm discussed in the previous section. You already know what is coming next, which will help you create transitions and ensure your paragraphs flow together.

Tip No. 66 **Print out or write down your thesis statement and outline for easy reference.**

These days, many students do almost everything digitally. If your outline is digital and your thesis statement is embedded in your introduction, you will have to toggle between windows on your computer to see your outline or scroll up to your thesis. This makes it difficult, if not impossible, to compare them side-by-side. To save yourself some hassle, print out your outline or take a few moments to jot it down in a notebook. You might want to consider writing your thesis statement on a notecard or sticky note and keeping it somewhere visible on your desk or even on the corner of your computer monitor.

Coherency is also a big concern with research papers. Papers that lack coherency are easy to spot because they jump from point to point and often leave the reader feeling confused. Following your outline will make sure your paper does not feel disjointed. This is not to say you cannot make any changes to your outline. You might find that switching the order of your paragraphs makes for a stronger argument or a clearer logical progression from one idea to the next. If that situation comes up, make the changes. Make sure changing the outline makes your paper easier to follow while still covering all your points. Whenever you reorder paragraphs, or even sentences within paragraphs, reread them for coherency. To accommodate the change, make any necessary adjustments whether they are adding a new transition or changing the wording to make it less confusing in the new context. Transitions will be covered more thoroughly in the next section.

Flow neatly from one topic to the next

Transitions are an important but often forgotten topic. Good transitions between paragraphs are another small set of details that separate a mediocre research paper from an excellent one. So, what exactly is a transition, and how do you use it effectively? Transitions are words and phrases that help a paragraph flow into the paragraph that follows it. Good transitions let the reader know the paper is changing to another point without catching him or her off guard. Transitions can be subtle or direct, but if they are absent, your paper will feel  choppy and disorganized. Transitions add coherency to the body of your paper and make it much easier to read.

Direct transitions rely on a transitional word or phrase to signal to the reader the topic is changing and give some clue about the relationship between the point of a paragraph and the one that preceded it. Nevertheless, additionally, similarly, first, last, and furthermore are all words that are direct transitions. Transitional phrases, such as "on the other hand" and "despite the fact that," can be used as well.

The following is an example of a direct transition taken from an analysis of Freud's research on Coca:

He also devotes time to discussing other medical uses of coca, such as treating stomach problems, long-term use for diseases that involve the degeneration of tissue, treatment of morphine and alcohol addiction, the treatment of asthma, use as an aphrodisiac, and use as a local anesthesia.

On the one hand, he does cite the use of coca as experienced by several different people, which is good because it helps eliminate the possibility of different people having widely varying reactions to the drug. He experiments with different potencies of his solution and explains that different doses have different effects on different people based on their tolerance...

The words "on the one hand" transition the reader from the list of the medical uses that Freud discusses at the end of the first paragraph to the analysis of his actual experiments. A phrase like "on the one hand" is generally followed by the phrase "on the other hand" and a contrasting point.

Subtle transitions also link the new paragraph to the one before it, but they do it indirectly. To write a subtle transition, take a few key words from the last sentence of the paragraph before the transition and work them into the opening sentence of the new paragraph. This creates a link between the information in the reader's mind and shifts to a new point without feeling abrupt or creating confusion.

The following is an example of a subtle or indirect transition taken from a paper about morality in epic literature:

```
Funeral rights and being able to have
a proper hero's burial for warriors who
died in battle is an important cultural
value, as shown through Beowulf's grand
funeral at the end of the epic. Grendel
devours his victims, so this is not even
an option. He is an instrument of death
and destruction, which shows that these
more physical concerns are the major
manifestations of evil in the world
of Beowulf.

   The portrayal of evil in Beowulf is
fairly straightforward and leaves little
question as to what is and is not evil.
Evil also does not masquerade as anything
else, which is a large difference between
the villains in Beowulf and the villains
in Spencer's The Faerie Queene.
```

Notice how the last sentence of the first paragraph contains the words evil and *Beowulf*. The beginning of the next chapter also uses both of these words but changes the focus from the manifestations of evil in *Beowulf* to the straightforward nature of this evil in comparison to *The Faerie Queene*. The topic changes, but by using points brought up at the end of the previous paragraph to start the next one, the train of thought flows smoothly from one topic to the next.

Both transition techniques are effective, and some paragraphs might lend themselves better to one or the other. The best papers will use a mix of both. Do what feels right. As long as the paragraphs flow together neatly, your transitions are working. If you have any doubts about your transitions, read the paper aloud and see whether you stumble between ideas. Alternately, have a friend look it over and give a second opinion.

CASE STUDY: ADVICE FROM A COLLEGE PREP TEACHER

Patrick Davey
Teacher
Lane Tech College Preparatory School
http://DaveyBio.yolasite.com

I have written college papers for all disciplines during my education at my university. They range from data-driven lab reports to poetry analysis. I also grade primarily college-level writing for my career as a college preparatory teacher.

Having quality resources is what separates a great paper from a mediocre paper. Wikipedia is not generally held as a credible source, but the links used as references in the articles can be. Always cross-reference your information as well. The problem with anyone being able to write anything is they do.

Being fluent in your writing and providing meaningful exposition is beneficial but without quality sources only produces a paper of fluff. Well-respected and relevant resources provide a necessary backbone to papers written at this level. In a research paper, you are not telling a person about a topic. You are explaining your argument to the reader. Keep asking yourself, "Why?" By answering this question over and over, you'll break down the topics so you do not leave the reader with any questions. Make sure your support ties to your thesis, and list where different sources you have available to you would fit best. The rest of writing the paper is just making connections.

Do not value another person's writing over your own. People value different styles, and it plays to the individual. Be original in your writing, and your professors will see your true skill and be able to give back the most effective feedback tailored specifically to you.

If you are having issues, take a seminar or reading a book on college papers. Expose yourself to well-written college-level papers so you know what to expect, and take advantage of the fact many papers at this level come with an objective rubric. Use it as a checklist to ensure a good grade.

Tip No.

67 Set goals based on output, not time.

It is no secret college students are busy. Finding time to sit down and write a paper between classes and extracurriculars can be difficult. Although it might be tempting to make plans to sit down and work on a paper for an hour and then do something else, this often leads to procrastination and until that hour is over. To increase productivity, set goals such as writing 500 words before practice or two pages before bed.

Study Guide

- The body of your paper consists of everything between your introduction and your conclusion. It is the largest part of your paper.

- The entire point of the body is to support the claims made in your thesis statement, so keep asking yourself, "How does this relate to my thesis?"

- Use cited research to support each of your main points.

   ◆ Do not skip putting in citations or put off inserting them until later. This will increase the chances you will forget a citation.

- If you absolutely have to skip adding a citation, make a notation that is easy to spot so you can find it again later.

- Follow every citation with an explanation of how this information supports or furthers your argument.

- You have room in the body for experimentation, but find a rhythm of citations and explanations.

  - Do not confuse getting a rhythm going with being boring or repetitive.

- Your thesis statement and outline should act as a map for writing.

  - If you get lost or find yourself wondering what to write next, refer back to your thesis statement and outline.

  - Keep a copy of each handy so you can refer back to them as often as you need.

- When possible, show readers rather than tell them information.

- Include transitions between every paragraph in your paper so they flow together neatly.

  - Transitions can be direct or indirect.
  - Vary your transitions to avoid becoming repetitive.
  - Use a few key words from the last sentence of a paragraph in the topic sentence of the next paragraph to link them together.

CHAPTER 10

Wrapping Things Up with the Conclusion

By this point, you should have finished your introduction and the body of your paper. The end is now in sight, which can be exciting and draining. It can be tempting at this point, especially if you are looking at a looming deadline, to quick write a few sentences that seem to wrap things up and call them a conclusion. Experienced and inexperienced writers alike can run into this problem, especially after marathon writing sessions. Fatigue sets in. Do not give in to the temptation to throw

something together that is just good enough. You spent a considerable amount of time and effort on this project so far, so why potentially throw it away now with a ramshackle conclusion?

The conclusion is the last thing your reader will see, so it should be memorable. A poor conclusion will leave readers feeling unsatisfied or as though they wasted their time. Even if the rest of the paper was well written, people remember the conclusion and will make judgments based on it. If you have ever watched a movie or read a book and been truly absorbed by it but were disappointed by the ending, you already know this. You likely walked away from the book or movie remembering what you did not like about the end rather than what you did like about the rest of it. No one wants readers to be left thinking, "What was the point?" or "Why did I even bother with this?" For this reason, make sure you give yourself enough time to properly write and edit a conclusion that complements the rest of your paper.

Tip No. **68** Trick yourself into allowing extra time to write your conclusion.

If you tend to procrastinate or budget all your time for writing the main body of your paper and run out of time for the conclusion, trick yourself into thinking you have less time than you do. Give yourself one deadline for everything up until the conclusion, take a break, then come back and take that extra chunk of time to write the conclusion. If possible, get everything else done one day early so you can spend the last day before your deadline writing the conclusion and editing.

Writing a good conclusion is simple, but it is not always easy. This might seem contrary, but quite a few things that sound simple require some effort. Rock climbing, for example, is not that difficult to explain, but it does require effort to complete. A good conclusion will review the key points of the paper and explain to the reader why the information is important, relevant, applicable, or related to the world as a whole. Although this does not sound complicated, many students balk at writing a conclusion or, worse, ignore it until the last minute and then do not put any time or effort into it. Succumbing to common pitfalls or rushing through a conclusion to meet a deadline can sour an otherwise well-written paper. The rest of this chapter will examine what makes a good conclusion and what to avoid while writing your conclusion.

Effective Conclusion Techniques

One of the easiest ways to write a successful conclusion is to take the same formula you used for your introduction and reverse it. Where introductions use an inverted pyramid structure, conclusions use a pyramid structure. Rather than start out with broad statements and then narrow to the thesis statement, a conclusion should do all of the following in this order:

1. Restate the thesis.

2. Reiterate the key points of the paper.

3. Explain why the paper is broadly relevant or what the reader should take away from the paper.

Conclusions: Pyramid Structure

If you read the Inverted Pyramid sidebar found in Chapter 8, this should look familiar. Use this thought process as a guide while writing your conclusion in the same way you did with your introduction. This time, the pyramid is right side up. The principle is the same, but the execution will be different. Your conclusion should start with a narrow statement that transitions the reader from the previous paragraph to the paper's main point. Once this main point has been re-established, give additional details to remind the reader of what they have read. Guide the reader from the specific focus of your paper to the broader considerations, such as how the research fits into a discipline, area of study, or the world as a whole.

Conclusions are written like **Pyramids**.
Introductions are written like **Inverted Pyramids**.

Do not get them confused. If it helps, draw yourself a diagram:

▼	Introduction
■	Body
▲	Conclusion

If you are a visual learner, note that the diagram resembles a wrapped piece of candy.

Restate the thesis

Restating the thesis is along the same lines as reviewing the key points of the paper, but it deserves its own section because many students have trouble with it. The best way to start a conclusion is by restating the thesis of your paper. Restating is not the same as repeating, so do not just copy and paste the thesis straight from the introduction. Although you certainly can start there, you need to change the structure and wording. This will keep you from sounding repetitive and show your mastery of the topic.

Tip No. **69 Avoid sounding apologetic.**
A common mistake made in conclusions is using phrases like "I am not an expert, but..." or "This paper has tried to show..." Using these phrases makes it sound as though you are apologizing to the reader for flaws and inadequacies in your paper. This is never acceptable. You need to leave the reader feeling satisfied and as though he or she learned something by reading your paper. Be firm in your conclusion just as you were in the introduction.

The restated thesis should address all the same points as the thesis and have an air of finality. You are not telling the reader what you are going to attempt to prove this time; you are telling him or her what you have proven through the research presented in the paper. The first step in doing this is rewording the thesis statement to remove any references to what will be discussed. Everything has already been discussed, so the tense should reflect this. Once you make sure the tense is appropriate, vary your word choice so it hits on the same major points but is different enough that it sounds fresh.

Review or reiterate key points

Tip No. 70 Dig up rough drafts and notes to get inspiration for your conclusion.

Odds are good that if you have done everything suggested in this book, you have rough drafts of thesis statements, topic sentences, and outlines. Consider keeping these documents in a folder, either digitally or in hard copy, so you can go over them later. You can polish wording that you scrapped the first time around and make a successful conclusion.

With the start of the conclusion out of the way, the next step is to review the main points from the paper. To start, look back at the body of your paper, or refer to your outline. Make note of the topic sentence of each paragraph. You can reword these sentences the same way you reworded your thesis statement and then incorporate that into the conclusion. This will quickly summarize the important details and keep you from spending too much time summarizing. Particularly striking quotations or statistics can also be repeated here, but do not use more than one or two. The conclusion represents your closing thoughts on the topic, so it should primarily consist of your own words.

In addition to summaries and quotations, conclusions could also contain recommendations to the reader or relevant questions that further the thesis. Ask yourself what you would ideally like to see readers do in reaction to your paper. Is there an action they should take or something they should examine or investigate further? Is there a bigger issue that your research draws attention to? Your reader will want to know the answer to these questions, so take a moment to reflect on what your ideal end results would be. For example, a paper on energy conservation might encourage readers to add eco-friendly practices to their lives. A research paper on a political proposal might ask readers to write to Congress and voice their opinion.

> **Tip No. 71 Create unity and wholeness in your paper by referencing your introduction in your conclusion.**
>
> By restating your thesis in your conclusion, you are already starting to achieve a sense of unity in the paper. Check whether there are other key words, phrases, or ideas that are mentioned in your introduction that fit into your conclusion. These can be subtle, but connecting the introduction to the conclusion in this way will help readers leave feeling satisfied. This is what it means to have your paper or argument come full circle.

Provide resolution

Although you can encourage readers to question their opinions or introspect on the bigger picture your topic is a part of, do not leave loose ends. You need to provide a sense of resolution, so make sure your conclusion wraps up your argument. Consider rereading the body of your paper and making a note of any details you feel the conclusion should touch on to make the paper feel complete. You also can keep a running list of these details while you write. Do not underestimate readers or assume they will not notice one or two forgotten details. Even if they cannot explain exactly what is missing, readers will feel somehow unsatisfied with a paper that does not provide resolution.

Tip No. 72 End your conclusion with something memorable, such as a question, warning, or call to action.

The conclusion of your paper should address one important question the reader will likely have: "Why should I care?" Ending your conclusion with a broad question that causes readers to consider how to use the information they have learned is one way of resolving this. Depending on the topic, ending with a warning or a call to action are also options. By warning the reader of something that might happen if people do not take notice of the issue you are covering or by asking the reader to step up and do something to change a situation, you have given them a reason to care and a possible way to use the information contained in your paper.

Traps to Avoid

Now that you understand what makes a good conclusion, it is important to understand which common mistakes students make while writing conclusions. Even if your conclusion meets the criteria listed previously, some errors will weaken or ruin a conclusion. The following sections will explain some of the most common traps students fall into and the ways to avoid them.

Too much summarization

Although summarization is a key part of any conclusion, it is not the only aspect of a conclusion. Many students make the mistake of rehashing what they already stated in their papers and then trailing off. These conclusions are weak because they do not leave the reader with a sense of resolution. Summarization is necessary to remind the reader of the main points, but this alone does not give readers a sense of what to take from the paper.

Explaining how to apply the information covered in the paper is just as important as refreshing the reader on all the key points. Keep summarization to no more than half of your conclusion.

If you find yourself relying on too many summarizations, make any of these statements more concise without losing important details. Once you have whittled down your summarization as much as possible, list the reasons that make your paper important. Look at these points, and see whether any of them can translate into questions or statements to pose to the reader.

Introduction of new information

Another common mistake students make is introducing new information in their conclusion. It is easy to do accidentally, especially when giving the reader a sense of how the information in the paper applies to the world at large. You can pose questions or explain how the information is relevant, but do not introduce key points that were not previously addressed in the paper. If you find yourself introducing new information at this stage in the writing process, stop and ask yourself why this

information was not included earlier in the paper. If it seems important, go back to your body and add the information there. If it is not important enough to earn a mention in the body of the paper, it does not deserve to be included in the conclusion.

Tip No. 73 Do not use your conclusion to make up for inadequacies in the body of the paper.

When you find you have not covered all the information in your paper that you originally intended to, the temptation is to throw whatever you missed into the conclusion. These conclusions are problematic because they do not conclude anything. They do not wrap up a paper; they only introduce more questions. This often happens when students do not narrow their topics enough. If you find you have information that has not been covered by the end of the paper, consider readdressing the scope of the paper to something more narrow.

If you have information you meant to include in the paper but left out for whatever reason, the topic you chose might be too broad. Determine whether there is a pattern or common theme to the information that you are introducing into the conclusion. If so, see whether you can rework your thesis so this extra information is not necessary. An excess of unused information might also indicate a lack of focus, so reread your paper for cohesion. If you are not sure of what, if anything, to leave out, ask a tutor for help.

Sample Conclusion

The following is a sample conclusion from a paper about Neo-Pagan religions and how they are adapting to modern technology:

> Many modern Pagan practices are quite
> different from what is believed to be
> the traditions of ancient Pre-Christian
> religions, but there are still
> similarities. Several of the differences
> that some modern Pagans embrace have been
> adapted from these ancient practices to
> make them more applicable to the modern
> world. The emphasis on individualism
> within the various Pagan traditions
> lends itself to adaptability, which is
> one of the numerous reasons Paganism is
> still surviving in modern cities and
> urban environments. Many Pagan practices
> are also similar to other major, or

more mainstream, world religions. This, combined with the fact that so many people are familiar with the lore surrounding the ancient pantheons of gods, makes converting to Paganism easy for those who desire to. Although it remains true that many ancient Pagan practices are not completely compatible with the modern world, the creative and devout still find ways to commune with nature in local parks and draw energy from power lines and water pipes. The Neo-Pagan movement is evolving into a religion with the capacity to thrive in a fast-paced, technologically driven, urban world, possibly even more so than several mainstream religions.

CASE STUDY: GREAT CONCLUSIONS MAKE FOR GREAT PAPERS

Matt Sias
Student
University of Wisconsin - Eau Claire

During college, I wrote and edited many research papers related to psychology. I also wrote and edited technical documents and step-by-step instructional documentation. Additionally, I have experience writing and editing public policy and financial legislation. Beyond that, I have studied, and frequently exercised, written interpersonal communication.

Great papers tend to have interesting and thoughtful introductions and conclusions. Papers that are not as good only include out of necessity an introduction and conclusion that add nothing to the worth of the paper. Great papers also have a logical progression and smooth transitions. It is easy to tell whether the author has reviewed the order of topics. Transitions are the key to helping the reader understand the author's ideas and, therefore, must aid the reader in moving from one topic to the next.

Use library employees to help research and interpret the meaning of any findings. Put your pen to paper, and write a rough draft. Ask your peers, instructor, and other people available as a resource to critique it. Spend time polishing the paper; you might go through many drafts. If you feel stuck, ask for help.

A good thesis statement outlines main points clearly and often takes a stance on the topic of the paper. Do not leave the readers guessing what the paper will cover.

Make the reader care about your topic. You do not need to write an introduction in the style of a speech with a shocking statistic or rhetorical question. Write to your audience.

This can be accomplished through the previously mentioned methods, but it can also be accomplished by making your topic relevant to the reader.

Great conclusions revisit the main topics in a way that is different from the rest of the paper. Do not list the points that were discussed. Do not introduce any new facts or information in a conclusion that was not mentioned earlier in the paper. Calls to action or thought-provoking statements make for a strong finish.

Study Guide

- Be sure to leave yourself enough time to write a proper conclusion. Tacking on a few sentences at the end of your paper is not acceptable.

- A good conclusion will do all of the following:

  - Restate the thesis.
  - Summarize the paper's main points.
  - Explain how the topic fits into the big picture or what the reader should take away from your research.

- The most common way to start a conclusion is by restating the thesis. However, restating does not mean repeating.

- Gather the main points the conclusion should review from the topic sentences and outline.

- If you have rough copies of topic sentences or thesis statements, use them to get ideas for your conclusion.

- Ask yourself what you would like the reader to do after reading your paper. If there is a point you want them to consider or an action you want them to take, make that obvious in the conclusion.

- The conclusion should be written in pyramid structure, the opposite of the structure used in introductions.

- Try to incorporate words and ideas from your introduction into the conclusion to bring the paper full circle.

- Avoid these common traps:

  - Do not spend too much space summarizing or rely on summary alone in your conclusion.
  - Do not introduce new information in the conclusion.
  - Do not attempt to make up for inadequacies in the conclusion; go back and fix the problem in the rest of the paper.

CHAPTER 11

Formatting and Reference Pages

With the conclusion out of the way, it is time to put the finishing touches on the research paper before proofreading and editing. In the hustle and bustle of finishing a major project, it can be easy to neglect or entirely forget about details such as formatting, but making sure the paper is formatted correctly is important and should not be forgotten. You also need to allow yourself enough time to compile your reference page. Do not make the mistake of thinking you can ignore your reference page until the last  minute. Reference pages can be time-consuming, so allow yourself enough time to compile your references.

The following sections will give you the tools you need to ensure your paper is formatted correctly and your reference page is properly compiled. There are countless ways to format a paper. The same can be said for reference pages. Each type of source has its own rules for proper inclusion in a reference page. Entire books have been dedicated to understanding formatting and citations for the various writing styles. These are known as style guides, and it is highly recommended you invest in one. It is not possible to adequately address every aspect of this topic in one chapter, so instead this chapter will give you a basic understanding and show you which tools are available to make this step of the writing process easier.

Formatting the Paper

Formatting refers to the general layout and appearance of a written document, in this case your paper. This includes the font, font size, spacing, alignment, margins, headers, and footers. MLA, APA, and Chicago Style all have different requirements for formatting. Your professor might impose additional requirements based on personal preferences.

> Tip No.
>
> ## 74 Formatting is part of the editing process.
> It can be easy to forget the formatting of your paper is something you likely will be graded on. For this reason, double-check your margins, fonts, headings, charts, and diagrams to make sure they are consistent and uniform and they look good on the page. Most professors and writing styles have requirements for margins and font sizes, so check these details before calling your paper done.

Finding formatting requirements

The first step in ensuring a paper is properly formatted is checking your assignment sheet or class syllabus for any instructions. Most professors will include which font, font size, spacing, margin sizes, and other details they prefer. In some cases, they might just require the paper be written in standard MLA, APA, or Chicago format. If this is the case, check a style guide, either online or in hard copy if you have one, for this information.

How to adjust the format

Your word processor should be equipped with the tools you need to properly format your paper. If you do not have access to Microsoft Word or a similar program on your computer, consider downloading a free one, such as OpenOffice. OpenOffice can be downloaded from **www.openoffice.org** However, by using a program like this, you might run into formatting issues when you transfer the document between OpenOffice and Word. You should also double-check your file extensions to make sure you are saving in a format that can be read by multiple programs, such as .doc.

The tool bar at the top of your word processing screen in Word will be all you need to complete basic formatting tasks. When changing the format of text that is already written, be sure to highlight or select all the text you are altering. Once the text is selected, you can use the options on the tool bar to change the font and font size and adjust the typeface to bold, italicized, or underlined. You can also use the alignment buttons to center information on the page. Alternatively, all of these tools can also be found under the Format tab.

The Format drop down menu is also used to adjust the line spacing and margins. To change the line spacing, open the "Paragraph" menu. Under the "Indents and Spacing" menu there should be a drop down menu called "Line Spacing." Use this to change from single to double spacing. Likewise, Page Setup, also found under the Layout tab or under the File tab on some versions of Word, will allow you to change the margin width on the top, bottom, left, and right sides of the page. The location of these options vary slightly from Windows to Mac and between versions of Microsoft Word. If you cannot find these options in your version of Word, use the program's help feature to find where these tools are located. In OpenOffice, many of these options reside under the format drop-down menu.

The majority of papers you write will be written in Times New Roman, 12-point font and be double-spaced with left alignment, so consider making these the default in your word processor to save time.

Headers and Footers

You might be required to include a header or footer in your paper with certain information in it. These are sections at the top or bottom of each page that include information such as the author's name, the page number, or the title of the work. Inserting these into your document is simple. In OpenOffice, access header and footer options under the format drop-down menu. In most versions of Word, the header and footer option is located under the View tab. However, in the Windows version of 2007, double-click at the top and bottom of the page to add headers and footers, or access these options in the header and footer group under the insert tab. If you have difficulty, reference your program's help menu.

One thing to note, however, is headers and footers will contain the exact same information on each page of the document. If you need to put a page number in the header or the footer, you cannot type the number in on each page. Instead, use the page number drop-down menu in Word under the Inset tab. In OpenOffice, expand the insert menu and choose fields. The fields drop-down menu has a page number option. If you cannot find this feature, check the help menu for information on how to do this in your program.

Tip No. **75** Give the paper a once-over while holding it upside-down.

This tip is especially important for papers that include visuals, such as charts, graphs, or pictures. Looking at the paper upside-down will make it easier to spot formatting or placement issues, such as incorrect font sizes, poor spacing, and margin errors. It is also easier to tell whether something is off-center if you look at it upside down and right side up.

Reference Pages

Reference pages are easily one of the most complicated parts of writing a research paper. Each style has a different way of including information in the reference page. They also call the reference page by different names. Each different type of source, including books, magazines, websites, and interviews, has a different format and different information that will need to be included in the entry. For this reason, either obtaining a copy of the style guide for whichever style you will be using most frequently or making use of free online style guides is extremely important. Regardless of how daunting or frustrating putting together a reference page might seem, it must be included in every research paper.

Tip No.

76 Always include as much information as possible on your sources.

Long-form citations call for all sorts of details about the source. These vary widely depending on the type of source, but you likely will find yourself in a situation in which a citation asks for more information than you have available on the source. Your source might not have obvious pagination, or you might be missing a publication location, for example. In this case, it is acceptable to leave this information out of the citation. But do not use this as an excuse to be lazy with your citations. Always be sure to include as much information as you can.

What is a reference page?

A reference page, also called a works cited page or bibliography, is a detailed list of all the sources used in a research paper. This is generally the last page in any paper. Regardless of the style, the purpose of the in-text citations is to direct readers to the reference page so they can look up information in the sources you used if they so choose. The reference page should contain enough information that the reader can find the exact source you used.

Works Consulted versus Works Cited

You might be requested to put together what is called a works consulted page. This is not the same as a works cited page though the format for the citations will be the same. A works consulted page is meant to include all the sources you read while doing your research that are *not* used in your paper. If you are required to include a works consulted page, be sure to take detailed notes of all of the sources you look at.

The importance of reference pages

The importance of citations is discussed in detail in Chapters 6 and 7. Even if you provide an in-text citation for every piece of information you include, your citations will not be complete unless they lead the reader to a matching entry on the reference page. If you do not provide a reference page or your reference page is not done properly, you might find yourself in trouble for plagiarism, falsifying information, or interpolating. Interpolating occurs when a person inserts new material into a text, particularly when he or she is using someone else's words to make a point. This is done purposefully to put words in an author's mouth and manipulate information, but it can happen accidentally as well. This is why knowing the difference between quoting, paraphrasing, and summarizing is so important.

Rather than give a list of all of the hundreds of types of citations, the rest of this chapter will instead provide information on where to go to find the format for citations in MLA, APA, and Chicago or Turabian style and offer an example of what a reference page in each style might look like.

Tip No. **77** Make a list of all sources cited in your paper, and compare that with your bibliography.

Depending on the format of your in-text citations, this can be tricky. Parenthetical citations are easier to spot than footnotes. Nonetheless, double-check your in-text citations to make sure they are included in your bibliography or works cited page. This is especially important for long research papers that require a plethora of sources. It can be easy for one to slip through the cracks, so keep a list handy of all the sources you used so you can cross-reference that with your bibliography.

MLA Works Cited

A reference page in MLA style is called a works cited page. This page will have the title "Works Cited" centered at the top. It will then list all the sources you have cited in alphabetical order. If the citation takes up more than one line, indent all other parts of the citation. Information for MLA citations can be found in detail at **www.mla.org** or on the Purdue OWL at **http://owl.english.purdue.edu**.

Sample

<u>Works Cited</u>

Archer, Shirley. "For Heart Rate, Tai Chi Comparable to Brisk Walk." IDEA Fitness Journal 5.3 (March 2008): 78(1). Academic OneFile. Gale. Carthage College/WAICU. 23 Apr. 2008 <u><http://find.galegroup.com/itx/start. do?prodId=AONE></u>.

Hardy, Annabel, Alice Solomon, and "Ki Treatment: Healing with Sound and Touch." Positive Health Magazine 142(2007):

National Center for Complementary and Alternative Medicine, "Tai Chi for Health Purposes." NCCAM Backgrounder. June 2007. National Center for Complementary and

```
Alternative Medicine. 25 Apr 2008
<http://nccam.nih.gov/health/taichi>.

Mayo Clinic Staff, "Tai Chi: Improved
    Stress Reduction, Balance, Agility
    For All." Mayo Clinic. 15 Nov 2007.
    Mayo Clinic. 25 Apr 2008 <http://www.
    mayoclinic.com/health/tai-chi/SA00087>.

Allen, Mark. "Tai Chi Do." Tai Chi Do. 25
    Apr 2008 <http://www.taichido.com/chi/
    home.htm>.
```

Tip No. **78 Double-check all your citation punctuation.**

Misplaced periods and commas are not worth losing points over. Though the details vary depending on which format your paper is in, most citation requirements have strict punctuation guidelines. It might seem silly or unimportant, but every little punctuation mark counts.

APA Reference Page

A reference page in APA style is called a Reference Page. This page will have the title "References" centered at the top. It will then list all the sources you have cited in alphabetical order. Though the format of the individual citations will be different, the presentation is identical to MLA style. Information for APA citations can be found in detail at **www.apa.org**, or on the Purdue OWL at **http://owl.english.purdue.edu**.

Sample

References

Archer, S. (2008). "For heart rate, tai chi comparable to brisk walk". *IDEA Fitness Journal, 78*(1), Retrieved from **http://find.galegroup.com/itx/start. do?prodId=AONE**

Hardy, A., & Solomon, A. (2007). Ki treatment: healing with sound and touch. *Positive Health Magazine,* 142.

National Center for Complementary and Alternative Medicine, (2008). *Tai chi for health purposes* National Center for Complementary and Alternative Medicine. Retrieved from **http://nccam.nih.gov/ health/taichi**

Tai chi: improved stress reduction, balance, agility for all. (2008). Retrieved from **http://www.mayoclinic. com/health/tai-chi/SA00087**

Allen, M. (2008). *Tai chi do.* Retrieved from **http://www.taichido.com/chi/home. htm**

Tip No. 79 Double-check the order of sources in your bibliography.

Depending on the assignment, you might be asked to divide your sources up by type or topic, but this is rare. Most commonly, sources are listed in alphabetical order within the bibliography. Make sure you have ordered your sources properly. Failing to do this will make your bibliography more difficult to navigate for you and the reader.

Chicago or Turabian Bibliography

If you are required to do the majority of your papers in Chicago or Turabian style, purchase an up-to-date copy of the Chicago Manual of Style and reference it often. You could also bookmark **www.chicagomanualofstyle.org** though this will require registering for the website and paying a subscription fee. There are multiple accepted methods for composing the Chicago/Turabian reference page, also called a Bibliography.

Tip No. 80 Be consistent.

Do not get creative with fonts, margins, and sizes throughout the paper. Keep it simple, easy to read, and consistent so the reader can follow along. Be sure to double-check formatting and abbreviations for consistency. Also, do not mix and match methods from more than one paper format. For example, if you use MLA parenthetical citations, you cannot use APA citations in your works cited page.

As with MLA and APA styles, you will be putting the title "Bibliography" centered at the top of the page. Endnotes are the most common method used. When using end notes, be sure to include a number at the front of each bibliography entry. This number should correspond to the superscript number assigned to that source within the paper.

> **Tip No. 81** **If you are struggling with putting together a reference page, ask for samples.**
>
> It can take time to get the hang of an unfamiliar style. Online citation makers can help, but they only go so far. If you are confused and overwhelmed, ask your professor or your school's writing center whether they have examples you can look at to help you figure it out.

Sample

Bibliography

1. Archer, Shirley. "For Heart Rate, Tai Chi Comparable to Brisk Walk." *IDEA Fitness Journal* 3, no. 5 (2008): Academic OneFile. [Database online.]

2. Hardy, Annabel, Alice Solomon. "Ki Treatment: Healing with Sound and Touch." *Positive Health Magazine*. 2007, 142.

3. National Center for Complementary and Alternative Medicine. "Tai Chi for Health Purposes." NCCAM Backgrounder. Available from http://nccam.nih.gov/health/taichi. Internet; accessed 25 April 2008.

4. Mayo Clinic. "Tai Chi: Improved Stress
   Reduction, Balance, Agility For All."
   <u>Mayo Clinic</u>. Available from <u>http://www.</u>
   <u>mayoclinic.com/health/tai-chi/SA00087</u>.
   Internet; accessed 25 April 2008.

5. Allen, Mark. "Tai Chi Do." <u>Tai Chi Do</u>.
   Available from <u>http://www.taichido.com/</u>
   <u>chi/home.htm</u>. Internet; accessed 25
   June 2008.

Tip No.

82 Do not forget to proofread your works cited page or bibliography.

Many students proofread their papers from introduction to conclusion and then neglect their compiled citations. Professors and graders will read them and dock points for errors here just as much as anywhere else in the paper, so do not forget to give it a once-over.

Study Guide

- Formatting is important. Make sure you are aware of any specific formatting requirements, such as margin width, line spacing, and font size, your professor or style guide requires.
- If you are having issues figuring out how to adjust the formatting, check the help guide in your processing program.
- Be sure you have a word processing program that has all of the features and formatting adjustment tools that you need.
  - If your computer does not come with the Microsoft Office Suite and you cannot afford to purchase it,

you can download a free comparable suite from **www. openoffice.org**.

- A reference page is a compilation of all of the sources you included in your paper. All your in-text citations should point to full citations in your reference page.
- Each style is different, so purchase a style book or bookmark an online style guide for more details on how to compose a reference page in the three major styles.
- Using an online citation maker, such as **http://citationmachine.net**, can save time though be sure to check them for accuracy before submitting your paper.
- Making your reference page as you write helps you avoid missing citations. If you choose to do it last, make sure you have notes with citation information for all your sources. This is especially important for long papers with many sources.
- Do not forget to proofread your reference page. Each style has its own particularities, and you do not want to lose points just because you put a comma in the wrong place.

CHAPTER 12

Proofreading and Editing

Proofreading is the last step in writing a phenomenal paper. As with prewriting and outlining, editing is an all-too-often neglected step of the writing process. Because this is the last step, poor planning often leads to students running out of time to edit. Some college students finish a paper ten minutes before it is due and turn it in still warm from the printer but later spot errors they can no longer change. Other students will only run their paper through the digital spell-checker in their word processor and

then call it edited even when they are not pressed for time. If either of these sound like you, now is the time to break yourself of these habits. If this is difficult for you, treat your papers as though they are due a day sooner than they are so you can give yourself time to polish them. There are two main categories of editing. There is editing the content, and there is proofreading, which is editing the mechanics. Both are equally important.

Tip No. 83 Take a break before beginning the editing and proofreading processes.

Realistically, this is not always possible. Late night crunches happen to even the most organized students, but allow yourself some time to relax before beginning the proofreading process. Walking away from the paper will give you some distance from what you have written, which will make it easier to spot mistakes. Get up for a glass of water, grab a snack, take a short walk, or watch an episode of your favorite TV show before diving into the editing process. This will give your brain some time to cool off so you come back to the paper refreshed and sharp.

Reading for Content

Tip No. 84 Editing is not just about spelling and grammar.

Do not forget to read your paper for clarity, focus, word choice, and other content issues before turning it in. Leaving out important details is even worse than making mechanical errors, and spell-checkers will not catch these types of errors.

This is the first type of editing, Reading for content does not focus on the spelling and grammar but on the actual content and substance of the paper. This type of editing is well beyond the capabilities of a spell-checker. Because editing for content will likely result in you changing, adding, and subtracting parts from your paper, doing this before reading for spelling and grammar is best. This way, you do not miss mechanical errors in any of the rewritten sections of the paper. Editing the content of the paper is not terribly difficult once you know what to look for. With practice, it can be completed quickly and easily.

Tip No.

85 If you were not provided with a rubric, you can make your own.

Many professors will provide students with a rubric, or a breakdown of what is expected for an assignment and how it will be graded. If your professor did not provide you with one, you can make your own by summarizing the assignment requirements and then using this checklist as you proofread and edit your paper. You can even ask your professor what he or she is looking for in the assignment and which aspects might be weighted more heavily. Include this in your notes.

Thesis properly supported

How long has it been since you looked at your thesis statement? Depending on the length of the research paper, you have likely spent anywhere from an afternoon to several days writing the body of your paper. Once their writing builds momentum, few people stop and look back at what they have already written. For this reason, some students will barely glance at their thesis until it comes time to restate in  the conclusion. This can lead to students leaving out key points mentioned in the thesis or not giving enough support to a point that they might have forgotten was included in their thesis.

Tip No. 86 Highlight sentences that answer your paper's key questions.

Remember way back before you started writing when you were asking yourself the who, what, where, when, why, and how of your topic? One way to edit your content and ensure you have not left out any key points is to make a list of these questions and then highlight sentences in your paper that address each. You can even highlight different questions in different colors so you can see whether specific areas need more support or are focused on more heavily than originally intended.

The easiest and most effective way to ensure you have properly supported your thesis is to get out your thesis and break it down into its main points. Once you have this list, go through your paper one paragraph at a time and check off each of the main points as you find evidence in your paper that supports them.

Once you have completed this, check whether any points are either unsupported or under supported. If this is the case, you have two options. You must either rework your thesis statement to make it fit the information the paper covers or you must add more supporting information to the body of your paper. Both methods can work equally well. Use your best judgment to decide which is more appropriate.

Tip No. **87**   **Consider using group study sessions to edit and polish your paper.**

Many writing intensive courses require students to break into small groups to brainstorm or peer edit. Too many students blow these off and do not use them as the resource they are. If you have friends in your class or find a group of like-minded classmates, set up times to meet and exchange ideas. It can be helpful to e-mail each other copies of your papers so everyone can look them over and make notes. The peer comments will improve your paper, and helping edit another writer's work will improve your writing as a whole.

If your argument is clear, seems to make a logical progression, and does not feel incomplete, you might be better off reworking your thesis to fit the paper instead of adding more information. If you are unsure of what to do, enlist the help of a friend. Ask him or her to make sure the progression of your argument is logical and point out any areas of the paper that seem unclear or confusing. Consider his or her suggestions, and make the appropriate changes. Of course, there are other factors to consider, such as how long rewriting the paper would take versus how much time is left before the deadline. You might also want to consider whether changing your paper would require additional research. The length of the paper might also be a factor. Rewriting a two-page paper will take considerably less time than rewriting a ten-page paper. Use your best judgment, and evaluate which is the best option based on the time and resources available.

Tip No.

88 Use the track changes feature when asking friends to edit your paper or when working on group projects.

Another feature that too few students are aware of is track changes. Most word processing programs have this type of feature, so see the program's help menu if you are having trouble locating it. Track changes will highlight and document all changes that are made to a document, which is helpful for group projects. It is also a way to learn from the editing process. Having a friend or tutor use track changes when proofreading your paper will let you know exactly what they changed, and it also gives you the option of either accepting or rejecting the changes they suggest. Keep in mind, however, that switching between different programs with this feature, such as different versions of Microsoft Word or Word and OpenOffice, might cause formatting errors. This can happen even when the programs are the same but is more common when switching between different programs or operating systems. Also, be sure to save your files in a format that can be easily read by multiple programs such as .doc or .rtf.

All research objectives met

The second part of reading for content is to make sure you met all your research objectives. If each part of your thesis is well supported, you are already halfway to meeting your objectives. The other half is making sure all the requirements listed in the assignment are successfully completed.

89 Use any online resources your college or class might have.

Many colleges provide websites for different courses. These websites have general information, helpful links, and assignment requirements on them. If your classes have these tools available, bookmark the links so you have this information at your disposal wherever you go.

Reread the assignment sheet. Find notes you might have from when the professor assigned the paper. If you sat down and discussed the assignment with the professor, make note of everything he or she mentioned. Make a list of all the requirements for the paper. This includes formatting requirements, source requirements, and page length.

Tip No. 90 Before calling your paper finished, be sure to review the requirements of the assignment.

It can be a letdown and a source of stress to find out at the end of writing a huge paper that you missed one of the assignment's requirements. Making sure you understand every aspect of an assignment before starting is important, but always be sure to read the assignment again once you have finished to reassure yourself you covered everything. It is better to find out now that you need to go back and add details than to find out when you get your grade.

Before submitting your paper, be sure you review this list and double-check that you completed everything on it. This might seem simple, but it will prevent you from making simple, easily fixable mistakes that will cost you points. Failing to do everything required in the assignment, no matter how minor, will change the way the professor or grader looks at the assignment. Even if the mistake was honest, whoever is giving you a grade might assume you did not read the assignment carefully enough and might judge everything in your paper more harshly because of it.

Tip No.

91 Save early, and save often.

Do *not* forget to save your paper. If your program has a tool to automatically save work, make sure to enable it. Even with that enabled, you should still save your paper whenever you take a break. Make backup copies on a flash drive, external hard drive, in your e-mail inbox, on your cell phone, or some combination of these. Few things are more stressful than losing hours worth of work because of a computer crash, so do not let this happen to you.

CASE STUDY: EDITING TIPS FROM THE WRITING CENTER

Jean Preston
Director, Writing Center, Adjunct
Assistant Professor of English
Carthage College

I have a bachelor's degree in English and a master's degree in creative writing and poetry, so I have written *many* college papers, including two major thesis projects. Since then, during the past six years, I have taught general education college courses and several other writing-intensive college courses. Therefore, I have extensive experience grading college papers.

To properly edit a paper, be sure you understand the assignment and the instructor's expectations. Use any resources available — a writing center, instructor office hours, a writing handbook — to help accomplish college-level writing.

Talk to a library research specialist about the process he or she is currently using that is unsuccessful so ineffective patterns can be identified, and be open to learning new skills to become more successful. Again, take advantage of the resources that are available and often free at the college.

Sixty percent of errors can be found by reading a paper out loud. Sentence-level errors are more easily found by reading the essay sentence by sentence from end to beginning. Proofread several times and concentrate on different issues or errors each time. Keep an error log of your most common mistakes with methods for correction and examples of the right and wrong ways of doing things.

Be sure each paragraph has a solid topic sentence that reflects the thesis and that each paragraph sticks to its topic sentence. Textual support should be gracefully installed and thoughtfully analyzed. Check your conclusion as well. A good conclusion should restate the thesis, but it should also address why the conclusion, idea, or argument is important. Also, students often introduce an entirely new idea in the conclusion. I teach students not to do this.

Also, do not be afraid to go back and significantly change material when you edit. You could write your best introduction *after* you write the rest of the essay. Then, you can design the introduction to be interesting and informative and to better address the content of the paper.

Procrastination is probably the worst enemy of the college writer. Start a project early, and access any helpful resources available to you sooner rather than later.

Grammar, Spelling, and Mechanics

Tip No.

92 Read your paper aloud.

Reading out loud requires a higher level of concentration than reading silently. You will remain more focused on the words that are on the page, which will allow you to spot errors more easily and will also highlight areas that might be clunky or poorly worded. If you stumble while reading a section, consider changing it so it rolls off the tongue more cleanly. You can also have a friend read the paper out loud to you. His or her lack of familiarity with the paper will make the rough spots even more obvious.

Once you are satisfied with your paper's content, the next step is checking the spelling, grammar, and other mechanics within the paper. No one wants to get a lower grade because of a misspelled word or forgotten comma. Even students who struggle with spelling and grammar are capable of learning to proof their own writing, so do not fret if mechanics are not your strong suit.

Proofing for errors in basic grammar and mechanics

Tip No.

93 Proofread with a screen.
In this case, a screen is a piece of paper or folder you lay over the document you are reading so you can focus on one line at a time. Plain white paper can work just fine for this technique. Use the screen to cover everything below the part you are reading, and then move the screen down as you read to reveal more of the document. This forces you to read more slowly and focus on each individual line, which will allow you to catch more errors.

There are several tricks when it comes to proofreading a paper. Many of them seem silly, but techniques such as reading a paper out loud or reading the paper from a print copy,do make errors easier to spot. Another technique is to read the paper backward. This can be done by either starting from the end of the paper and reading each sentence, one at a time, from the end back to the introduction. This takes the sentences out of context, which will help prevent your brain from going into autopilot. You can also read each sentence backward starting from either the beginning or end of the paper. For example, "Read each sentence backward," would be read as, "backward sentence each read." This forces you to look at each word individually, which will make misspellings easier to spot. Try a variety of these techniques to find which ones work best for you.

Tip No. **94** Print your paper out, and read it.

For whatever reason, many people find it easier to spot errors on a hard copy. It might seem like a waste of paper, but if you find yourself constantly missing typos and other errors, print your paper out and step away from the computer. Mark it up with a red pen, and then take it back to the computer to make the changes. Cross them off on your hard copy as you go.

If you know you have trouble spelling certain words or correctly using grammatical conventions, make yourself a cheat sheet to keep by your side as you read your paper. You can then reference this whenever you come across one of your trouble spots or something else that does not look quite right.

Tip No. **95** If you find yourself making the same type of error over and over, make a note of it.

The more you write and edit your papers, the more you will start to notice patterns in your own writing. If you start to see these patterns yourself or if someone points out a mistake to you that you have made several times, write it down so you can remember it and avoid making it in the future.

The following tables can also be used as reference. They contain some of the most common errors people make when writing.

Common Mistakes	Correct Usage Explanation
Your and You're confusion	"Your" is a possessive word indicating ownership. (ex. Do not forget your bag.)
	"You're" is a contraction of the words "you" and "are." (ex. Are you sure you're going to come with us to the movie?)
Its and It's confusion	"Its" with no apostrophe is the possessive form of the pronoun "it." (ex. The dog wagged its tail.)
	"It's" is a contraction of the words "it" and "is." (ex. It's hot out today.)
There, Their, and They're confusion	"There" is used to indicate a place. (ex. Do not park there.)
	"Their" is the possessive of the pronoun "they." (ex. We got here in their car.)
	"They're" is a contraction of the words "they" and "are." (ex. They're bringing the car.)
Comma splices	Comma splices occur when two complete thoughts are improperly joined with a comma, which creates a run-on sentence.
	"We decided to go to the movies, we saw the new comedy film" is a comma splice and can be corrected by placing either a period or a semicolon in place of the comma or putting a conjunction such as "and" after the comma.

Common Mistakes	Correct Usage Explanation
Pronoun Disagreement	Pronoun disagreement occurs when a pronoun does not correctly match the noun it replaces. This most commonly occurs when a plural noun is being used.
	"Your professor will tell you what they want in the assignment" is an example of this. The pronoun, "they," is plural, but the noun it is referring to, "professor," is singular.
	This can be corrected by either changing "professor" to "professors" or by changing "they" to "he or she" if the gender is unknown or choosing either "he" or "she" if the gender is known.
Tense Disagreement	Tense disagreement occurs when a shift is made between past, present, or future tense for no reason.
	The sentence, "When she drove to work, she goes past the gas station" is incorrect. The section before the comma is in past tense, but the part after the comma is in present tense.
	To fix this, either change "drove" to "drives" or change "goes" to "went."
Improper Semicolon Use	The semicolon (;) is one of the most misused punctuation marks. Semicolons are used to join two complete thoughts that are closely related.
	They are not a replacement for commas or for a period if the two thoughts are unrelated. A semicolon can take the place of a comma and conjunction when it is joining two complete thoughts. It can also take the place of a period that separates two complete but related sentences. (ex. We went to the movies last night; we saw the new comedy film.)

This is not a complete list, but it is a starting point. If other mechanics rules give you trouble, add them to this table.

> **Tip No. 96 Read your paper in reverse (Or: reverse in paper your read).**
>
> By this point, you have likely read and reread your paper dozens of times, which makes proofreading problematic. You have read the material so much that you miss errors because you subconsciously change what a sentence says to what it should say. Starting at the back end and working your way to the front is a way to avoid this. To proofread for spelling, look at your paper one word at a time backward. For grammar, do the same thing but read by sentence.

Using automated grammar and spell-checkers

> **Tip No. 97 Do not rely on spell-checkers to edit your paper.**
>
> In a digital age during which so many basic tasks are automated, it can be easy to rely on your computer's spelling and grammar checking functions to do your editing for you. Although these tools do make it easy to spot misspellings and other errors, they are far from foolproof. Do use these tools, but still look the paper over with your own eyes to catch misplaced words or spelling errors the computer misses.

Automated spelling and grammar checks area blessing and a curse to students. These tools are standard in word processing programs and will catch the majority of spelling errors and even some grammatical errors depending on the sophistication of the software.

Although these are helpful because they make errors easy to spot, they will miss things. For example, if you mistype a word but the error happens to be the correct spelling of another word, the spell-checker will not flag it. For example, if you tried to type "gear" but accidentally hit the "F" key, which is next to the "G" key on a standard QWERTY keyboard, you will spell "fear." Depending on the context, spelling and grammar checks likely will miss this. Mistakes like this happen frequently, so be sure to keep your eyes open for them. Even when a word is flagged as a misspelling, it can be easy to click on the wrong suggested word because most of the time, the program will make several guesses about what you meant to type. Some of these programs will even attempt to automatically correct errors or predict words as you type, which is useful until it automatically corrects a misspelling to the wrong word without your notice. In short, these tools save time but they are not a replacement for reading over a paper with your own eyes.

Tip No. 98 Add technical words to your word processor's dictionary.

Depending on your subject, you might find terms that your computer does not recognize. Spell-checkers will catch chemical compounds, proper nouns, and other jargon even when they are spelled right. Be sure you do have the spelling right, and then add these words to your word processor's dictionary. This will make it easier to avoid misspelling these words throughout the paper.

Other Resources for Polishing a Paper

Tip No. 99

Make yourself aware of dictionary functions and other helpful tools on your computer.

Computers are wonderful tools even when you are not using them to their fullest potential. Most computers and computer programs come preloaded with features that make writing and editing much easier. One of these functions is the dictionary tool, which will allow you to look up the definition of an unknown word. The dictionary function might also include thesaurus information, which is useful when editing out trite phrases and overused words.

If your campus offers on-site writing help or access to tutors, book an appointment to get help with editing your paper. These resources are almost always free and will vastly improve your writing in a short amount of time. If you have a paper due during a busy time, such as midterms or finals, be sure to book an appointment well in advance because they fill up quickly.

Tip No. 100

Use the "find" function in your word processor to help you edit quickly.

Most word processors have an awesome feature called "find" or "find and replace." This tool can make some types of editing much quicker and easier. For example, using the find feature to locate all apostrophes in a document will highlight any contractions that you might have accidentally used. If you tend to overuse particular words, you can use "find" to locate them and make the appropriate changes. Consider making a list of words you know you want to avoid using, or over-using, and then search your document for each of them. This is a quick way to improve your paper.

You also might consider looking into software that can analyze your word use frequency. These programs will take a text, analyze it, and then make a list of the most commonly used words in it. This, combined with a thesaurus, will improve your writing and your vocabulary. Programs like this can be purchased or downloaded from the Internet either for free or a small price. A good example of a web-based application can be found at **http://rainbow.arch.scriptmania.com/tools/word_counter.html**. Hermetic Systems also has a program that you can download from their website at **www.hermetic.ch/wfc/wfc.htm** that will analyze word frequency. There is a trial of the program available, or you can pay for the full version. These are only two examples. A quick search of the Internet should point you in the direction of several more programs and websites and plug-ins you can install with your office suite to make them capable of analyzing word frequency. Just be aware that many of the online applications can only analyze up to a certain number of words, and analyzing a huge document could cause the website to timeout. Because of this, these applications are better suited to smaller research papers than full dissertations.

Tip No. **101** Relax, and congratulate yourself on a job well done.

You have reached the finish line. Your paper is done, still warm from the printer, and ready to turn in or possibly already in the hands of your professor. Do not stress out about the grade you will receive; move on and focus on the next assignment. Even if you do not do as well as you hoped on this assignment, treat it as a learning experience. Ask yourself what you can do differently next time, and take constructive criticism to heart.

Study Guide

- There are two main types of proofreading and editing. These are editing for content and editing for mechanics, spelling, and grammar.

- When proofreading for content, highlight sentences that answer your paper's key questions.

- Consider using group study sessions to edit and polish your paper. Your friends will catch errors that you might miss.

- Use the track changes feature when asking friends to edit your paper or when working on group projects.

- Do not call the paper finished until you review the requirements of the assignment and make sure the paper meets them all.

- When proofreading for mechanical errors, do the following:

  - Print your paper and read it.
  - Read your paper aloud.
  - Read your paper in reverse.
  - Do not rely on a spell-checker to edit your paper.
  - Proofread with a screen.
  - Use the find and replace function in your word processor to help you edit quickly. This is useful for finding overused words and replacing them.

- Always take a break before beginning the editing and proofreading process.

- Check your formatting and the way the paper looks on the page, too.

  - Holding the paper upside-down can help with this because you will catch layout errors you otherwise might miss.

The Road to Success is a Rocky One

As with most things in life, learning to write well involves a large measure of trial and error. Some students will find the writing process comes easily once they learn the basics. Others will struggle with developing a style and learning how to construct a strong, logical argument. Even students who have natural writing talent make mistakes and experience pitfalls that come from a lack of experience. Knowing what professors are looking for and, more importantly, how to find out what professors want to see is just as important as your skill level.

Students who have a history of producing well-written and highly praised papers in high school will still struggle in college if they do not understand what their instructors are looking for. Standards are higher in college, and impressing graders is just as much about being able to say something novel and different as it is about being able to say something well. There will be ups and downs, as each instructor likely has personal standards and expectations that you will have to adapt to. A paper worth an A grade for one professor might only be the quality of a B grade to another.

The important thing to remember is that writing great papers is a *skill*. It is something that you can learn how to do though it might take a lot of time and hard work. The best and only way to improve your writing is by practicing. With each assignment you complete, you will get better. If you do not do as well on one assignment as you had hoped, learn what you can from the experience so you will have more skills at your disposal next time. Over time, you will find adapting your writing to fit different academic situations will get easier.

In the end, you will be glad you acquired these skills regardless of your major or field of study. With the globalization of society and prevalence of the Internet, e-mail, and other digital communications, being able to write well is more important than ever. The skills you develop in college by researching, compiling and condensing information, formulating a well thought out argument, and expressing your thoughts and ideas clearly on paper are valuable skills that will serve you well no matter where life takes you.

CASE STUDY: SENIOR ADVICE

Megan Hammer
Student
Carthage College, German Major

The most recent thing I wrote was my thesis — the big final project everyone has to complete before graduating. It was hard because few books have been written in German about translation, which was the topic of my thesis. I struggled with the assignment, and I did not always see eye-to-eye with my professor. For example, being told I *had* to use this book or that book in my paper was a challenge because I had *no* idea how to fit a book about philosophy into a paper about translation.

This project was a huge undertaking, and I was told to rewrite nearly from scratch about three times. I kept all my drafts, though, and I was able to copy and paste parts of older versions into the newer ones. I spoke with another professor when I was struggling, and it helped solidify ideas in the areas that were giving me the most difficulty. I also talked my ideas over with my aunt, and she kept asking me questions until I had refined the basic idea from "about translation" to the easier topic of "translation and culture."

A computer crash caused another huge setback. I was lucky enough to be able to recover all the documents from my hard drive after my computer's untimely death, but not everyone is that lucky.

My best advice is as follows:

Research early, and research often. Any time you see something that *might* be useful, write the quote down on a notecard with the source on it. Then, even when you don't have the book anymore, you still have that quote you think is useful.

Focus on getting to the core of what you want to say. You might need to write three pages of fluff before you get there, but as soon as you get to your point, you know it, and you can move all that fluff into another word processing document. You never know when you might need filler. Be passionate about what you are writing about, but make it clear and easy to follow.

Expect edits, so do not to take it personally when your first and even second drafts are torn to shreds. If you are struggling and the pressure is getting to you, take a step back from it for a day. Talk it out with someone you know will be honest with you, and look at your failures and accomplishments. When I started doing that, I felt as though I was getting a lot more done.

I met with a friend in my thesis class every Monday night for two hours, and we would work on our papers together at that time. I was lucky my other classes did not take so much time outside class that I couldn't focus mainly on writing.

The best way to get used to writing is forcing yourself to write. I overcame the pressure of writing papers in a short amount of time by participating in National Novel Writing Month. I then knew I could write 50,000 words during a month because I had already done it. After that, writing a 20-page thesis and editing it in four months seemed much less daunting.

Don't write it the night before it is due. And although you might be a sarcastic person in real life, that isn't the best thing to be in the academic world, so keep your writing professional and your own thoughts and remarks out of your paper.

Don't expect to get along with every professor you have. Sometimes, nothing you do will be good enough for one of them. Learn to focus on your accomplishments, not the downfalls, and accept help in whichever form it might come.

Save often, and make backups on places other than your computer. You never know whether your computer will die three days before your thesis is due.

Sample Research Papers

The following are two sample research papers. The first was written for a class about Asian and American cultures. The second was written for a class on world religions. The first one is annotated with highlights of specific things the student did well and explanations of the structure of the paper.

The second one has room for you to try your hand at annotating the paper by either making a copy of the pages or writing directly in the book. See whether you can recognize the parts of a research paper and the aspects of it that are done well. Being able to recognize these things will go a long way toward improving your own writing.

Both of these papers are presented in MLA format though the citations could easily be changed to comply with other styles.

Erika Eby

Name Of Professor

Course Title

Date

◄ This heading will contain your information. Check your style guide for heading formats.

Anime and Social Issues: A Method of Exploration for a New Generation

Culture and the various issues present in a society are always intertwined. Culture, especially popular culture, is a means of measuring social morals and standards at any given time, as well as an embodiment of the ideals of the populous. Although pop culture is defined by our society, it is also largely what defines our social issues. Being influenced largely by the media, global or otherwise, pop culture is often fluid while, at the same time, deeply ingrained in our psyche and social norms. Because of this, few things are as powerful at documenting social issues as the forms of entertainment a group of people generates for themselves, such as film, music, television, and literature. The themes and social commentaries portrayed in these cultural artifacts are often just as fluid as the culture that generates them. More recently, the technology humans immerse themselves in on a daily basis has become a major theme found in many of these cultural commentaries, Japan's anime being no exception. <u>Anime (and manga, its comic book counterpart) is a growing genre of entertainment, particularly popular with younger audiences, that explores pressing social issues, be it in cyberpunk stories, such as Serial Experiments</u>

◄ The thesis statement for this paper is underlined. Notice how it explains the topic without revealing the whole argument.

◄ This information is a paraphrase and is cited as such.

Lain; family movies, such as Princess Mononoke; or romantic comic books, such as Chobits.

Anime comes in many flavors, from "shōjo" or "little girl" anime to post-apocalyptic fantasies. Animated shows can be found on television in Japan throughout the day, from children's shows in the morning to family shows during the evening, as well as the edgy late-night programming aimed at older teenagers or 20-year-olds (Napier 16). Because of the diversity it displays, it appeals to a wide range of people and can be found covering a wide array of topics and genres. One theme found in a variety of anime and manga is the effects of technology on society. Chobits by CLAMP, a shōjo manga, focuses on the relationship between humans and "persocoms," robots programmed to act and do tasks like humans. Princess Mononoke, a family-focused anime, explores the delicate balance between nature and a world being destroyed by human technology and pollution. It should be no surprise, then, that technology and its effects on society is a major theme in "cyberpunk" anime, which is a genre classified as dealing with both highly advanced technology and some sort of degradation of social order. Serial Experiments Lain (1998) by Yoshitoshi ABe[1] is a perfect example of a graphic artist in the cyberpunk genre who is fairly well-known in both Japan and the United States.

Though MLA format does not usually employ end notes, the author has included one here to explain the capitalization.

Lain is slightly different, stylistically, from much of what is considered popular anime, as the colors are more muted and the physical features of the characters are less exaggerated, but its selling power rests more in the complex social issues it grapples with throughout the course of the 13-part miniseries. The series brings up questions about identity, reality, communication, and the role of technology in the modern world. Not only does it do this in "not-too-distant-future" setting, it also incorporates several pieces of gadgetry that echo current technology. For example, much of the plot of Lain centers around "The Wired," a cyber world very much like an advanced version of the Internet. The computer that the protagonist, Lain Iwakura, owns is called a "Navi" and looks very similar to an iMac. It is small details such as these that not only record what current pop culture standards are, but also comment or satirize them as well, or, in the case of Lain, invite viewers to draw their own conclusions and make the commentary themselves.

◀ **Here the author uses an indirect transition.**

The fact the Lain creates a world in which it is possible to look more objectively at our own culture and make comparisons is one of the main reasons why it can effectively deal with issues such as technology in our culture and get at the deeper significance. The importance of abstracts such as reality and identity in Lain are key to not only following the complex plot of the series, but also to getting the value out of the series. Lain does not have a clear message or a moral that comes out in the end; rather, it is a complex social commentary that has many layers of meaning and is meant to be interpreted by the audience. In fact, the episodes of the series are actually referred to as

"Layers." The series itself starts with a schoolmate of Lain's committing suicide, but it focuses on Lain and the people she comes into contact with as well as the different aspects of her personality that end up splitting into their own individual entities. This split becomes more noticeable to the viewers once Lain modifies her computer to make it possible to completely project herself into the Wired, a cyber world with borders that are starting to bleed into that of the real world. Lain starts to see the blurring borders of these worlds after she receives an e-mail from her dead classmate who claims that by committing suicide she only abandoned her body and now lives in the Wired.

From there it becomes more and more clear that there are at least three different versions of Lain, which she refers to as "different mes." One is the Lain of the real world, or the childish and naive part of her who still sleeps in teddy bear pajamas; one an outgoing party girl, who dominates the Wired; and one who is evil and manipulative. This split coupled with the blurring of reality not only expands the philosophical impact of the series, but also brings to mind questions about the reality of the cyber world created by the Internet. Lain believes that reality is within the mind of the individual, rather than something external: "People only have substance within the memories of other people. And that's why there were all kinds of mes. There weren't a lot of mes per se, I was just inside all sorts of people, that's all," Lain explains her justification for her alternate personas and brings up

◀ **The author leads sets up the quotation effectively with a brief explanatory statement, followed by a colon, and then the quotation. After the quotation, the author explains the quotation and how it relates to the argument.**

questions that the viewers have to attempt to answer on their own. This idea of reality being a self-contained and relative entity evolves into the central question that Lain struggles with. As she herself poses, if no one remembers something, did it ever exist to begin with? In that same light, if you remember something that never happened, who is to say it is not real? More pressing, though, in our modern culture, is the idea of personas and the difference between the digital world and the "real" world. With the advances in technology and communication, humans now have the ability to connect in ways never before imagined, but the social and moral questions brought up with virtual reality games on the internet are still being debated.

Games that allow users to create a digital avatar, or computerized versions of themselves, and then interact with other users in a virtual world setting are becoming increasingly popular around the world. "Second Life," created by Linden Labs is an online game currently popular in the west where users create 3-D avatars and then interact with each other in a virtual world. Users can even buy land from the company or from each other, and the games economy has become so prosperous that the "Linden Dollar" is equivalent to a US dollar. The game already has some areas designed specifically for Japanese users, and the number of Japanese users is expected to spike over the summer when the game will introduce Japanese language software (Kono 4). Granted, even with this game users still cannot travel inside their computers, like Lain does, but the borders between what is real and what is digital are blurring in this way. Much in the same way all Lain needs is a Psyche chip to enter the Wired, all it takes is a free download from Linden Labs to join the "Second Life" community.

It is easy to claim that anime or manga in specific genres are the exception, however cultural implications extend beyond just anime and manga genres that are meant to critique society, such as cyberpunk. Some may get a different impression after watching episodes shows imported as Saturday morning cartoons, such as Pokémon and Sailor Moon, but it is important to remember that these imports are usually watered down versions of their original counterparts. Some of the same questions that are raised by Serial Experiments Lain are raised by Chobits, the shōjo manga by CLAMP. Shōjo is a genre characterized by young female leads, such as Sailor Moon and Chobits. "Shōjo" literally means 'little female' and originally referred to girls around the ages of 12 and 13. Over the last couple of decades, however, the term has become shorthand for a certain kind of liminal identity between child and adult ... a consumer culture of buying 'cute' (kawaii) material goods ..." (Napier 118). The term is rather elastic and far-reaching, however, so it is hard to define. Chobits does fit into this category due to the cute and innocent, although robotic, female lead, Chi. While remaining very much that genre, Chobits also looks at the relationship between humans and technology, though it takes a different twist than that of Lain.

Chobits offers an inventive, slightly futuristic world in which computers have evolved into "persocoms," androids that look almost identical to people, except with larger, almost catlike ears, for storing connection wires, and all the hardware of a computer. There are also smaller, doll-like computers that function similar to PDAs or palm pilots. Because persocoms function much like normal humans, they are often programmed to perform human tasks and behave similar to humans. This development alone raises questions about the relationship between humanity and technology, especially how humans and technology that has advanced to this level should interact. The idea of creating technology that imitates and may be uncontrollable by humans is by no means a new one, and it is often explored in various media because it is a subject too close to home to be examined any other way. Manga, such as Chobits, can "depict fantastic and otherwise impossible scenes, making the stories and images 'safe' for exploration without, in theory at least, either disrupting or being disrupted by the real world," (Izawa 140). This is especially true of the persocom Chi, found by Hideki, the male lead, because she has the capacity to love and to feel.

Throughout Chobits' story arc, many of the characters struggle with some sort of realization about the robotic persocoms that they surround themselves with and the individual uniqueness, or personality, that each persocom has. In the case of Hideki, he struggles with both his feelings for his persocom, Chi, and her mysterious past as he found her abandoned and reset in an alleyway. When he manages to turn Chi on, he realizes that she does not function like a normal persocom and does not seem to have an operating system installed. Through talking to several authorities on persocoms he begins to wonder if Chi is one of the legendary Chobits, persocoms able to think independently of their programming and feel human emotions. Eventually, Hideki is confronted by the previous owner of Chi, who just so happens to be his neighbor, Chitose Hibiya. He finds that Chi is indeed a one of the legendary persocoms and was created by the man who invented persocoms for his wife, Chitose, because she was unable to have children. He created two, Elda (later Chi) and Freya and gave them the ability to fall in love. Freya had her heartbroken and malfunctioned as her programming could not handle the emotional load, so Elda copied Freya's memories into herself, erasing her own. Hideki eventually discovers that Chi has chosen him as her special someone and freezes all other persocoms until he chooses whether or not to accept her love. He struggles internally with his feelings for Chi but does come to terms with the fact that he is in love with her, and Chi then gives her gift to all persocoms, the ability to feel and be happy.

Even though Chobits is a shōjo romantic comedy, it still covers some of the same issues as Serial Experiments Lain. Where Lain struggles with her identity both in and outside of the Wired, the humans, especially Hideki, in Chobits are confronted with the idea of robots having identities and feelings, as well as the idea of considering them real people. Chi also struggles with redeveloping herself after her memories were erased. Freya's memories are still in her programming, so she has some guidance from her acting almost as her conscience. Chi also has to grapple with finding her "someone just for me" or her true love, which is closely attached to her sense of self and is a very human rite of passage. At the same time, though, she is not human and so the humans who come into contact with her, like Hideki, have to constantly wonder if she is actually perceiving the world and acting on her emotions or if she is simply being driven by her programming.

Although many of the issues presented in Chobits may seem far fetched, the truth is that humanoid and highly advanced robots are reality, especially in Japan where most of these technological advancements are being researched. Recently, SGI Japan Ltd. has developed a robot with software that recognizes patterns in the human voice to detect emotions. The robot reads the voices of people talking and then projects colors into the room based on the emotion. It can be programmed to project calming colors when speakers get angry or excited and also recognizes command phrases (Nakamura). Humanoid robots are also slowly gaining new abilities, and, in doing so, are becoming more life-like. The University of Tokyo is currently researching robotics to develop humanoid robots that could serve in factories or homes. They are working with seven major companies "to merge robotic technologies with information technologies." $8.4 million a year will be spent on the project, making more versatile humanoid robots with a wider variety of motor function (Matsuda). Although these robots do not have the versatility of the persocoms described in Chobits or the ability to feel, as Chi does, we are certainly moving in that direction.

Chobits is not the only more mainstream anime to comment on these social issues that may have a lasting effect on our future. Hayao Miyazaki's Princess Mononoke is more of a family movie that features a sort of romanticized or reverent view of Japan's history and mythos. Princess Mononoke represents another face of the historical anime: the elegy. Mononoke tells the story of a prince who gets cursed while defending his village from demon and the journey he goes on while attempting to get the curse removed. He is told to go to a place called Irontown because they might be able to help him, but while going there, he gets dragged into a war between the people of Irontown and the nature spirits of the surrounding forest. Irontown was created as a sort of safe-haven for lepers and former prostitutes, but to maintain the town, they rely on the production of iron, which is destroying the forest. Because of this, the forest spirits, specifically a pack of wolf gods along with San (Princess Mononoke), a human female who was raised by them and hates all things human, are trying to kill the leader of Irontown. Because of this, the people of Irontown try to kill San, but Prince Ashitaka for some inexplicable reason feels compassion toward San and saves her, almost killing himself. Thus, San protects him from the human hating forest spirits. Now a part of this war, Ashitaka tries to help both the people of Irontown and San, because he feels that the war is being driven by blind hate. As the war rages and the head forest spirit is beheaded, it falls to San, who is now cursed as well due to a run in with a demon, and Ashitaka to bring back the head and stop the spirit from destroying the forest in its search. They manage to do so, and, once the spirit is reunited with its head, it restores the forest and removes the curse from both San and Ashitaka. Ashitaka then must stop San from attacking the humans of Irontown. San calms down, and though Irontown agrees to try to live in harmony with the forest from now on, San is still hurt and cannot live among the humans. Ashitaka stays with the people of Irontown but goes to visit San in the forest when he is able, and the movie ends with the forest regrowing.

This movie revolves around tension between history or the natural world and industrialization or technology. This is also the highest grossing Japanese film of all time, which shows how broad its appeal is to Japanese society (Napier 176). Films such as this tend to bridge the gap between apocalyptic anime and historical anime, as they often focus on the downfall of humanity due to the abandon of that which was once sacred and revered. In the case of Princess Mononoke, instead of idealizing the samurai era, the film hearkens back to a Japan where nature was revered as sacred and humans lived in Harmony with it. The artfully created tension between the ancient nature gods that supposedly once ruled and the human domination of the world turns from tension to a battle between humans and nature that is barely avoided. "It is a wake-up call to human beings in a time of environmental and spiritual crisis that attempts to provoke its audience into realizing how much they've already lost and how much they stand to lose," (Napier 180). It is arguably because these themes are so thought-provoking that Princess Mononoke is the top-grossing Japanese film of all time; why it has reached such a large audience beyond just children and beyond just Japan. The cinematic quality and complex themes are refreshing, especially from a medium as versatile as animation.

◀ This source was missing an author, so the citation includes the first part of the title. As long as it is still easy for the reader to locate the information in the works cited page, this is fine.

Princess Mononoke proves that not all anime that addresses social issues use futuristic issues that may seem unrealistic to make a point. Princess Mononoke uses a historical setting, and though there are many elements of fantasy to the story, much of it is also based in history. It addresses issues that are especially pertinent and close to home today due to environmental problems that are starting to surface. Humans are now starting to feel the effects of deforestation and global warming, and these will become the issues newer generations have to tackle. Pollution simply compounds this, as much of Asia is now realizing. The problems brought up by Princess Mononoke about industrialization and its effects on our environment are issues throughout the world, especially in Asia. Japan and China have recently begun negotiations to develop mutually beneficial strategic ties to boost economy and find ways to deal with increasing air pollution and other environmental issues ("Japan"). Although talks might not go quite in the direction Hayao Miyazaki had in mind with Princess Mononoke, the fact that Japan and China are even having negotiations proves that there is an issue and that anime is just one format that can be used to explore such issues.

◀ Notice how the author summarizes the key points, but also explains how this topic relates to the world as a whole.

Anime and manga is a growing genre of entertainment that explores pressing social issues, be it in cyberpunk stories, such as Serial Experiments Lain; family movies, such as Princess Mononoke; or comic books intended for little girls, such as Chobits. Though it does so through hand drawn cartoons that often have fantastic elements, it often makes social comments on issues that may hold stake in the future of Japan as well as the world as a whole. Because anime is hand drawn and usually has elements that make it seem different from reality, it allows people to explore their feelings on these issues in a way that feels safe because it allows for a barrier between fantasy and reality the same way over-the-top parody and satire does. Though many may say that pop culture is artificial and unimportant in relation to our future, anime disproves this because of the topics it covers, specifically topics that are rapidly becoming the issues that younger generations will be faced with. By confronting complex issues and making them accessible to a wide variety of people through varying genres of interest, it takes entertainment beyond just something to occupy time and into

◀ Here is the note referenced earlier.

something that allows people to reflect on themselves and draw conclusions about the state of the world in a safe environment separate from the drudgery of daily life.

[1] The capitalization of ABe is a personal preference of Yoshitoshi ABe when he writes his name in Roman letters.

Works Cited

Craig, Timothy J. Japan Pop! Inside the World of Japanese Popular

Culture. Armonk, NY: M.E. Sharpe, Inc., 2000.

Izawa, Eric. "The Romantic, Passionate Japanese in Anime: A Look at

the Hidden Japanese Soul."Japan Pop! Inside the World of Japanese Popular Culture. 2001.

Kono, Etsuo, Makoto Miyazaki. "Harsh realities of 'Second Life.'" The

Daily Yomiuri (2007): 4.

Matsuda, Shogo. "Humanoid Robots Gain Ability - Slowly but

Steadily." The Nikkei Weekly (2007).

Nakamura, Gen. "Robot Reflects Emotions in Backdrop Colors ." The

The paper closes with a properly formatted MLA works cited page. Notice how the formatting is consistent, the author gave as much information as was available on the sources, and she alphabetized them for easy reference.

Nikkei Weekly (2007).

Napier, Susan J. Anime from Akira to Princess Mononoke: Experiencing

Contemporary Japanese Animation. New York: Palgrave, 2000.

"Japan, China Launch High-Level Economic Dialogue." Japan

Economic Newswire (2007).

Erika Eby

Name of Course

Name of Professor

Date

Paganism in the Age of Information

Most people have been exposed, at some point in their lives, to relics of ancient religions, be it via tales of the escapades of the Greek and Roman pantheons or through learning about Egyptian mummification practices. There is something oddly captivating and awe inspiring about monuments such as the Parthenon at Athens and Stonehenge in Britain. Images of these relics along with Druid priests in long flowing robes and rural Shamans taking spiritual journeys are what often come to mind when people talk of Paganism. New Age revivals of many ancient Pagan spiritual beliefs, however, have put a modern twist on ancient Druidism and Shamanism. Entirely new religions have even risen from the revival of these ancient spiritual practices, such as Wicca. The modern urban and suburban culture may seem to undermine the simplistic lifestyle many think of in association with paganism, not to mention hinder the focus of these religions on the beauty and power found within nature. If nature is such a key part of Pagan beliefs, how is it that Paganism is not only surviving, but in some cases thriving, in the modern urban environments? Though the urban and suburban world, with its hectic nature and technological advancements, requires some adaptation to Pagan practices, the religions still honor and celebrate their ancient counterparts with a modern twist.

One of the most sacred parts of most Pagan religions is ritual and spell work. Spell craft in the modern Pagan perspective is different from the magic one might read about in fantasy novels. Rituals to honor the divine and the cycles of nature are comparable to a Christian attending church on Sunday. Going with that same metaphor, magic (or "magick," as some call it to distinguish it from stage magic) is similar to a Christian prayer. It is believed that if one focuses his or her desires, he or she can alter the flow of energy and make those desires manifest. The changes, however, are small things. "You're never going to shoot lightning from your fingertips, nor will you win the lottery because you lit a green candle. And you're certainly not going to become the Big Pooh-Bah of Magic because you picked up a copy of spells from some Big Name Pagan," (Beyer). Spell casting is often combined with ritual and is used for protection, healing, and divine guidance, not for putting "hexes" on one's enemies.

Many aspects of modern Pagan religions overlap with Christian traditions and holidays. This helps add to the allure of these New Age religions and is one of the many reasons modern urban people are starting to convert to Paganism. Many Pagans have the misconception that the reason for these similarities is because Christians desecrated and stole traditions from other Pre-Christian religions. This, however, is simply because of the way religions evolve and spread over time. "...Certainly the overlap of holidays and locations helped ease the transition, but it was not an overnight process, nor were the formerly pagan communities without a hand in all this. Religion is an evolving thing. Even when new ideas are accepted, old ones are not easily set aside like last week's newspaper, and the Church was wise in recognizing this fact," (Beyer). By the same principle, the reverse is proving true in modern culture. The similarities between Christianity and Paganism play a part in the effectiveness of modern Pagan movements, as well as Paganism's adaptability to the modern world.

Part of the adaptability that makes Paganism appealing in modern city-dwelling culture is the lack of universalized formalities and formal scriptures. There is no book that tells Pagans how to celebrate their holidays or how to worship their deities, so practices can vary greatly from practitioner to practitioner. There are some Pagans who feel there is a proper order and set of materials required to effectively hold rituals and perform spells, but there is also a growing number of Pagans who disagree and show ways to make magic simple and affordable. Kaldera and Schwartzstein are among them: "You have to have everything from the proper set of thousand-dollar robes to the right stuff in your stomach to a pharmacopoeia of obnoxious, illegal herbs and (ugh!) dried animal bits from obscure third-world countries...Sorry, wrong again. (Unless that kind of thing really turns you on.)," (Kaldera 9). If complex ritual is something that appeals to a particular Pagan, that is fine, but there are ways to draw on the energy and power of everyday items and junk found in the city as well.

Because of the idea that a Pagan does not necessarily need to spend a fortune on spell working tools, Paganism is evolving into a more and more "practical" religion, so to speak. City-dwellers who do not have time to regularly attend church or adhere to a strict religious timetable may find Paganism appealing. "Urban Primitives" is a term that is starting to be applied to Pagans who use the city for their religious workings. They adhere to the idea that much of ancient religious practices were about survival in a harsh environment, so adapted practices today should apply to survival in the urban environment. They may be strapped for cash and go dumpster diving for ceremonial tools or use common city weeks for spell work. With many of the principles of magic relying on the concept of directing energy and cities being places with lots of energy, it seems logical for there to be some Pagans who choose to harness this energy as well as the energy of the natural world (Kaldera 1-7).

By this same token, a growing number of practitioners of magic are abandoning their personal altars and elaborate ritual preparations and taking magic to the streets. Many believe that in today's world, asking for the help of the deities or focusing energy to create change should be able to be done "on the go" as needed. In other words, it should be able to be used practically. "If magic works, then it should work as well on the street as it does in the temple...Performing practical magic is an exercise in self-trust," (Dunn 139). There seems to be a call for, in today's society, a way to connect with the divine anywhere and to effectively take some sort of action and gain some control over an individual's own fate during the crazy ebb and flow of day to day life in the 21st century.

Many modern Pagans are also embracing technology in a way that other religions are not. Computers and the Internet are considered by some to be viable ritual tools or ways of communing with the divine. Technology is becoming an integral part of daily life, from computers to cars, and that is not looking to change. Anything that a person uses regularly starts to take on that person's personal energy, making it a powerful item. Many pagans also commune or "invoke" spirits or deities in their rituals, for example, calling upon a particular goddess or the elements for help. The elements can be contacted through modern incarnations of them according to urban Pagans. For example, phone lines and modems house air spirits, power lines are linked to fire, and plumbing or drinking fountains are linked with water (Kaldera 71-79). Going along with this line of thought, modems and the Internet are sacred to some.

Some Pagans take this a step further and actually hold religious ceremonies in chat rooms, in some cases. Not all Pagans do this, but some who live in isolated areas or who do not know others who they feel comfortable worshiping with in their area, find it easier to fit online ritual into their schedule (Kaldera 179-181). This has caused some tension in the Pagan community, as some feel that something as "unnatural" as the Internet should not be viewed as a divine medium. Others feel that their ancestors were focused on survival and would embrace the new technology. Regardless, the Internet is a widespread means for communication and for the sharing of information, which is integral to Pagan religions. "As the information superhighway embraces ever-increasing levels of intensity, I believe many magical devotees will feel powerfully drawn towards embracing the new technology in all its diversity. Sacred shrines and archetypal symbols will find a richer and mover convincing graphic expression on the Internet so that they really do become magical doorways in their own right..." (Drury 100). Despite the arguments for and against such use, the embracing of the Internet in some Pagan communities is an adaptation of these religions to better equip them for survival in the 21st century.

Even without the use of technology, many Pagans are starting to evolve the faces of their gods and goddesses to ones that are more helpful in day to day city life. Simple spells are performed to avoid traffic, and some may call on a deity to find a parking spot. These things may seem trivial, but to those who are trying to hold down a job, they can be important to survival. The idea of "triple deities" is important to Wicca and many other Pagan traditions. Deities of old such as Zeus, Artemis, and Loki are called upon by many to aid in goals or ritual work. On other occasions, one of the faces of a triple deity may be called on (i.e. The traditional triple goddess has three faces: Maid, Mother, and Crone). An example of an urban revamp of these deities would be the goddesses "Squat," "Skor," and "Skram" or the gods "Slick," "Screw," and "Sarge." Squat may be called upon to ensure a parking spot, Skram tells you when you need to leave a dangerous area, and Sarge is a god to help give you motivation to get a job done. This may seem silly and almost sacrilegious to some, but in Paganism, the focus is more on the energy that is in everything on Earth than the names associated with it. The tools and names used to call upon the divine, which is viewed as a manifestation of that energy, are just things to help the practitioners focus their wills and intents (Kaldera 55-68).

Many modern Pagan practices are quite different from what is believed to be the traditions of ancient Pre-Christian religions, but there are still similarities. Many of the differences that some Pagans embrace have come about as adaptations of these old practices in order to make them more applicable to the modern world. This easy adaptability due to the individualism emphasized within the various Pagan traditions is one of the many reasons Paganism is still surviving in modern cities and urban environments. Many of the practices are also similar enough to major religions, and most people have heard enough about the lore of ancient pantheons of gods to make converting to Paganism easy for those with the desire. Ancient Pagan practices may not be completely compatible with the modern world, but the Neopagan movement is evolving into a religion with the capacity to thrive in this fast paced urban world.

Works Cited:

Beyer, Catherine Noble. Wicca For the Rest of Us. 2002. Timerift Network. <http://www.wicca.timerift.net/>

Drury, Nevill. "Magic and Cyberspace." Esoterica 2002: 96-100.

Dunn, Patrick. Postmodern Magic: The Art of Magic in the Information Age. St. Paul: Llewellyn Publications, 2005.

Kaldera, Raven and Tannin Schwartzstein. The Urban Primitive: Paganism in the Concrete Jungle. St. Paul: Llewellyn Publications, 2002.

Helpful Links

Son of Citation machine
http://citationmachine.net

Purdue OWL (Online Writing Lab)
http://owl.english.purdue.edu/

Modern Language Association
www.mla.org

Chicago Manual of Style
www.chicagomanualofstyle.org

OpenOffice
www.openoffice.org

LibreOffice
www.libreoffice.org

Google Scholar
http://scholar.google.com

Google Documents
http://docs.google.com

Microsoft Academic Search
http://academic.research.microsoft.com

Citation Manager with add-on for Firefox
www.zotero.org

Refseek
www.refseek.com

Glossary

Abstract – An abstract, sometimes called a Précis or Synopsis, is a brief summary of an article, analysis, or other in-depth dissertation on a particular subject. Abstracts are often found at the beginning of scholarly articles to give readers a succinct overview of what the article will cover. Some large research projects might require students to write an abstract. An abstract generally includes an explanation of the topic, the research methods used, the results, and a hint of the conclusions drawn from the research.

Acknowledgment – A section, often in the beginning, of many books or other longer works in which the author credits others who have helped shape his or her work. This can be useful in research because it explains where the author drew help or inspiration and might lead to ideas for other sources to research.

Annotated bibliography – A bibliography that includes an evaluation or summary of each source listed. These are often used to ensure a student has properly researched a topic and validated all sources used.

APA style – Created by the American Psychological Association, this style guide is widely used in psychology and other social sciences. *For detailed* *information on how to cite sources and construct a bibliography using APA style, see Chapters 7 and 11.*

Article – A written piece that explores a specific topic. Articles are generally an independently written part of a periodical, such as a newspaper, journal, or magazine.

Autobiography – A biographical work that was written by the person who is the subject of the biography. These are primary sources and often offer insights that biographies do not, but some authors might exaggerate or bend the truth to make a better story, so their credibility should still be examined.

Bibliography – Sometimes called a Works Cited page, a bibliography is a list of all sources used in a research paper, article, or other document. The format of this will vary depending on the type of style being used.

Biography – A work written to contain factual historical information about the life and times of a particular person or persons. Biographies are secondary sources because they are not written by the subject of the biography. They are researched by an author and compiled.

Blog – An abbreviation for Web log, blogs are increasing in popularity and are widespread on the Internet. Blogs exist on almost any topic, but the anonymity of the Internet makes checking a blog author's credentials difficult.

Body – The bulk of any research paper, the body consists of everything between the introduction and the conclusion. The body of the paper should lay out the paper's main points and support the thesis statement with cited research.

Boolean search – A type of searching commonly used in search engines and databases. Boolean searches have three primary functions. "And," "Or," and "Not" are used to set the parameters for the search. Using "And" between keywords will return only results that contain both keywords. Using "Or" will return results that contain either keyword. Using "Not" eliminates any results that contain an unwanted term.

Brackets – In research papers, brackets are used to insert words into a quotation. Brackets should be used sparingly and only when additional context is needed for the quote to make sense. They are most commonly used to replace a pronoun with the noun it is referencing when that noun is not otherwise included in the quotation.

Catalog – Library catalogs organize and allow users to search for particular information. Catalogs used to consist of cards detailing information on each title in the library, but most libraries now employ digital catalogs. These allow users to search more easily and efficiently than they could with card catalogs.

Citation – A notation after a piece of research giving credit to the author or source that the information came from.

Citation guidelines – Several methods exist for citing sources. The three most common formats are MLA, APA, and Chicago/Turabian. These guidelines explain how to cite various sources so they are uniform and easily understood by the reader.

Conclusion – The last section in a paper. Conclusions start out by restating the paper's thesis and then broaden. The best conclusions will briefly recap the paper's main points while also explaining how they are applicable to the reader or the world or both.

Credibility – The trustworthiness of a source, or how reliable the information contained in a source is. *See Chapter 4 for more details on evaluating credibility.*

Cross-reference – Comparing and contrasting information on a subject from one source to information in a different source. This is a good way of checking the validity and credibility of information.

Database – An organized collection of information on one or more topics that is in digital form. Databases have largely replaced card catalogs in student research. Academic databases are a source of articles and other sources for research papers.

Dissertations – A written essay, paper, or other long compilation on a particular topic. This term generally refers to the piece of writing graduate-level students write to be awarded a doctorate. These can be sources for papers and are places to look for other sources pertaining to a particular topic.

Ellipses – Used in research papers to indicate something has been omitted from a quotation. They should be used sparingly and should never be used to change the context of a quote. They should omit information that is not pertinent to the topic of the paper.

Endnote – A note at the end of a document referenced by a superscript or subscript number within the document.

File – A digital collection of records or other data.

Footnote – An explanatory note or comment at the bottom of the page in reference to a particular piece of information contained on that page.

Foreword – A short introductory statement preceding a published work. These are often written by someone other than the author.

Glossary – A list of terms and definitions pertaining to a special subject or field of study.

Index – An alphabetical listing of topics found at the end of most books and other long documents. Indexes generally include all page numbers where a particular word, phrase, or topic is mentioned, which makes navigating a long work much simpler.

Interpolate – To introduce new information into a document or to otherwise alter a document. This term is generally used to indicate deceptive altering of documents or intentional misquoting.

Introduction – A short statement at the beginning of a work that explains what will be covered in the document. Introductions are often written by the author of the book, article, or paper. This can also refer to the first paragraph of a research paper.

Journal – A periodical published by or for a special group, profession, or organization. This term is also applied to newspapers, especially daily ones.

Keyword – A significant or defining descriptor in the title, summary, or text of a document.

Pagination – The number of pages in a manuscript or the way in which a manuscript's pages are marked to indicate their order.

Peer-reviewed article – An article, sometimes called a Refereed article, that was reviewed by other scholars in a field of study before publication.

Periodical – A magazine, newspaper, or other journal that is printed on a regular, periodic schedule.

Plagiarism – The unlawful or unauthorized use of the language, thoughts, or intellectual property of another author. Representing the work of another as though it were your own original work.

Précis – See Abstract.

Preface – An introductory section, generally used in a book or other longer work, that explains or introduces the topic and gives background information on the topic, author, or research. This is often, but not always, written by someone other than the author of the actual book or article.

Primary source – An original and authoritative document or eyewitness account pertaining to an event or subject.

Refereed article – See Peer-reviewed article.

Review – A critical evaluation of a document, book, or other work.

Rough draft – The first, unpolished version of a piece of writing

Scan – To glance over a document and survey it for important ideas that stand out to get an idea of the document's content.

Search engine – A program that searches documents, particularly on the Internet, for a user-defined keyword.

Secondary source – Any document that describes an event, subject, place, or thing that was not created at the time of the event or by an eyewitness.

Synopsis – See Abstract.

Thesaurus – A reference book of synonyms and antonyms.

Thesis – A proposition put forward in a research paper or other document that is then defended and argued by the author.

Transition – A word, phrase, sentence, or passage that links an idea or section to the idea or section following it.

Website – A connected group of pages on the Internet devoted to a person, organization, purpose, or topic.

Wikipedia – An Internet-based encyclopedia that allows anyone to add, delete, or revise its content.

Author Biography

Erika L. Eby is a freelance writer, editor, artist, photographer, and e-book author. She holds a degree in English with an emphasis in composition from Carthage College. A jack-of-all-trades, her writing experience covers a variety of topics, including opinion pieces, how-to  guides, reviews, promotional pieces, academic research, prose, and poetry. Her open and honest approach to writing makes her pieces easy to understand and relate to. She resides in Racine, Wisconsin. You can visit her through her website at **www.hijINKSstudios.com** or by e-mailing her at **MsErikaEby@gmail.com**.

Index

A

Abstract, 275, 280, 281

APA Format, 148-150, 157, 215

B

Blogs, 276, 72-74, 83, 97, 98

C

Catalogs, 87, 88, 277, 278

Citation methods, 135, 143, 144, 148, 277

Cliché, 169, 171, 172

Credible sources, 72-75, 81, 103, 182

D

Declarative statement, 52, 55

F

Footnotes, 132, 151, 157, 219

H

Headers and footers, 214, 216

Hook, 53, 57, 70, 161, 162, 175

I

Inverted Pyramid, 163, 176, 199, 200

M

Mechanics, 34, 39, 137, 227, 236, 237, 241, 245

MLA Format, 18, 145-147, 157, 184, 251, 253, 215

N

Narrowing the focus, 45, 47, 69

O

Organizing, 29, 40, 41, 105, 106, 110, 112, 123, 181

Outlining, 15, 57, 105, 111, 113, 116, 227

P

Paraphrasing, 120, 121, 128, 132-136, 181, 219

Plagiarize, 126, 127

Primary sources, 80, 83-85, 276

Proofreading, 213, 227, 228, 232, 237, 241, 245, 246

Q

Quotation outline, 112, 120, 122, 181

Quoting, 121, 128-132, 136, 181, 219

R

Reference pages, 213, 217-219

References, 40, 41, 72-74, 86-88, 96, 113, 124, 151, 157, 193, 201, 213, 221, 222

Revision, 51, 61, 63-67, 72-74

Rough draft 72-74, 209, 281

S

Secondary sources, 80, 83-86, 147, 276

Sentence outline, 115-117, 120

Style guides, 145, 214, 217

Summarization, 204, 205

T

Tense disagreement, 240

Topic outline, 114, 116, 120, 186, 210

Topic sentence, 120, 183, 185, 187, 195, 202, 235

Turabian Style, 148, 150, 151, 157, 219, 223